126 CACTI AND OTHER SUCCULENTS IN COLOUR

By the same author

The Complete Book of House Plants
Ideas for Your Garden in Colour

In the same series

201 Indoor Plants in Colour
    Rob Herwig

200 House Plants In Colour
    G. Kromdijk

WIM OUDSHOORN

Translated by
Marian Powell

126 CACTI AND OTHER SUCCULENTS IN COLOUR

LUTTERWORTH PRESS · GUILDFORD AND LONDON

Drawings: Marjolein Bastin

Photographs:
Auvimedia/Paul ter Straeten, Zoeterwoude: 35, 37, 46–1,
56–1, 61–1, 75–1, 88–1, 90–1, 107–1.
A. F. H. Buining, Leusden: 43.
B. van Gelder, Ruurlo: 55–r, 91–r.
R. Heij, Wageningen: 39, 96–1, 103–1.
A. J. de Looze, Rotterdam: 68–1, 78–1, 99–r, 100–1, 104–r,
107–r.
F. Noltee, Dordrecht: 49–1, 53–1, 54–1, 55–1, 70–r, 78–r,
80–r, 82–r, 88–r, 99–1, 101–r, 104–1.
Ing. W. R. Oudshoorn, Rijnsburg: 84–r.
Proefstation v. d. Bloemisterij, Aalsmeer: 68–r, 71–1, 80–1,
89–r, 100–r.
D. Smit, Amsterdam: 45, 46–r, 47, 48, 50–1, 52–1, 54–r,
56–r, 59–1, 60, 62–1, 63–1, 64–1, 67–r, 69–1, 72–r, 73–1,
74, 76–1, 81, 85–1, 87–r, 92–1, 93, 94–1, 95, 96–r, 102,
103–r, 105.
P. Stad, Wageningen: 33, 41, 49–r, 50–r, 51, 52–r, 53–r, 57,
58, 59–r, 61–r, 62–r, 63–r, 65, 66, 67–1, 69–r, 70–1, 71–r,
72–1, 73–r, 75–r, 76–r, 77, 79, 82–1, 83, 84–1, 85–r, 86,
87–1, 89–1, 90–r, 91–1, 92–r, 94–r, 97, 98, 101–1, 106.

First published in Great Britain in 1977

I S B N 0 7188 2305 2

Filmset by Keyspools Ltd., Golborne, Lancashire, Great Britain
Printed in The Netherlands

CONTENTS

INTRODUCTION

Cacti and other succulents have become fashionable. In our modern, centrally heated houses with their dry atmosphere, these plants normally feel perfectly at home, even though the light is often inadequate.

In recent years the demand from the public for greater knowledge of the subject has grown considerably, as is evident from the rise in membership of cactus and succulent societies. This book with its many clear illustrations in colour is therefore very welcome. It is important to know to which genus the various plants belong, since the conditions in which they grow in their native surroundings vary considerably. Their names form another fascinating subject for study. Many young collectors inevitably link the purchased plant with the name on its label and an amateur collector will find it easy to compare the plant with an illustration in colour. Nevertheless it should be borne in mind that the appearance of a young plant is often entirely different from that of mature specimens capable of flowering. In our climate the conditions in which the plants—as a rule propagated from seed—are grown are usually totally different from those in their country of origin. The fact that shape and spine formation of cultivated specimens differ to a fairly large extent from those growing in their native habitat, is frequently due to the intensity of the light and the amount of sunshine available. Photographs of specimens cultivated in this part of the world from reliably named seed are therefore important for the purpose of comparison.

Why one group of cacti should produce woolly hairs and a flowering zone (cephalium), while another flowers from practically bare areoles, remains a mystery which makes this plant family all the more interesting. The deeper one delves into the subject, the more one becomes fascinated by the cultivation of these plants. I hope, therefore, that in these restless times this book will encourage many readers to relax in their care and propagation.

A. F. H. Buining

WHAT ARE CACTI AND SUCCULENTS?

Let me start by correcting a misunderstanding concerning cacti and succulents.

All cacti are succulents, but not all succulents are cacti. Cacti form a separate botanical family, as do bromeliads, composites, etc.

The word succulent is derived from the Latin 'succulentus', meaning juicy or fleshy. All plants whose leaves, stems and/or roots are able to absorb and retain more than normal amounts of moisture are classified under this name. The ability to do this makes them better equipped than other plants to survive prolonged periods of drought. leaves and stems are transformed, thick and swollen, and consist of fleshy tissue. It should be remembered that bulbous and tuberous plants, such as tulips and gladioli, are also capable of absorbing and storing moisture, but in this case the reserves are confined to the underground parts of the plants.

Succulents occur in many botanical families. The only families consisting almost entirely of succulents are Crassulaceae (Stonecrop family), Mesembryanthemaceae ('Living stones' family) and Cactaceae (Cactus family). (Mesembryanthemaceae are sometimes treated as part of Aizoaceae). Among other well-known plant families with fleshy-leaved representatives are Euphorbiaceae (Spurge family), Asclepiadaceae (Milkweed family) and Liliaceae (Lily family). There are even succulent plants belonging to the Daisy family (Compositae), the Geranium family (Geraniaceae) and the Bromeliad family (Bromeliaceae).

This still does not explain the difference between cacti and other kinds of succulents. It is in fact quite simple. Cacti always possess so-called 'areoles', small, felted, cushion-like structures often, though not invariably, bearing thorns. Moreover, with very few exceptions cacti do not possess leaves, though they have thick, sappy stems or branches, frequently grotesquely shaped. The thorns that are nearly always present vary greatly in shape and size. It is to this feature that the cactus owes its name, for 'kaktos' is the Greek word for a kind of thistle, a rather prickly plant as we all know.

PROBLEMS OF NOMENCLATURE

In this book a large number of botanical names are mentioned which the layman often finds difficult, if not impossible, to pronounce. Our daily conversation does not contain words such as Glottiphyllum semicylindricum, Austrocylindropuntia verschaffeltii and Nopalxochia phyllanthoides, and it is therefore not easy to get used to them.

But is this necessary? Is there no other solution and could we not use popular names instead? The answer is yes and no. Popular names of course present no problem where our indigenous flora is concerned. Everyone knows what is meant by dandelion, or to which plant the name 'nettle' refers. Nevertheless there are regional variations and a flower called by a certain name in one part of the country may elsewhere be known by an entirely different name, so the matter is not as uncomplicated as one might think. Where cacti and other succulents are concerned the difficulty is that practically all these plants originate in distant countries. The majority come from the Americas and from Africa—not exactly next door. It would not be practical to use the popular names they are given in those regions—if, in fact, they exist at all.

Although some of the best books on cacti and other succulents published mention several popular names, these do not often tell us a great deal. What do you think, for instance, of names such as Bowstring Hemp, Creeping Devil or Lobster Claw?

Clearly it will be more convenient to use botanical names, which have many advantages, the greatest being their international character. The majority are Greek or Latin in origin and are in use all over the world. Botanical names, moreover, show the relationship which may exist between various plants, and finally these names frequently indicate a plant's special features or characteristics.

Let me give you a few examples. There is a particularly attractive succulent called Argyroderma testiculare. The first name includes the word argyreus (or argyreius), which means silvery, while testiculare may be interpreted as tuber-shaped. And this is quite correct, for the plant is silvery in colour and shaped like a tuber. Another example: Espostoa lanata is covered in woolly white hairs and this is indicated by the name, for lanata (from lanatus) means woolly. This botanical nomenclature was introduced by Carl Linnaeus, a Swedish botanist who lived from 1707 to 1778. It is called binary nomenclature. Each scientific plant name consists of a minimum of two words, namely the generic name and the specific epithet; only the former is written with a capital.

Take, for instance, the well-known cactus called Mammillaria. This is the generic name. There are numerous different kinds or species of Mammillaria, more than 200 in fact, and each of these has its own individual name. Hence we speak of Mammillaria schiedeana, M. zeilmanniana, M. spinosissima and so on.

Often the species are further subdivided into varieties or forms. When these occur naturally, they have additional names, beginning with a small initial letter like that of the species but prefixed 'var.' or 'f.', e.g. M. spinosissima f. rubra. If, however, the strain has arisen in cultivation or is normally maintained artificially, it is termed a cultivar. The supplementary name is then written with a capital letter and enclosed in single quote-marks or prefixed cv. An example would be Aeonium arboreum 'Atropurpureum'.

Argyroderma testiculare

Another simple example: This book mentions a plant called Sedum sieboldii 'Mediovariegatum'. Sedum is the genus to which the plant belongs; the species is called sieboldii. The specific name is essential to distinguish it from other Sedum species (e.g. Sedum acre, S. nussbaumerianum, S. palmeri, S. lineare, etc.). The name 'Mediovariegatum' indicates that we are not dealing with the species in the form in which it normally grows wild in Japan, but with a selected type that has leaves with a yellow blotch in the centre.

In the course of centuries many plants have, moreover, frequently been crossed with others; this is often done with cultivars, sometimes with species (e.g. Echeveria 'Derosa', the result of crossing Echeveria derenbergii and Echeveria setosa). Occasionally two genera have been crossed; an example is × Pachyveria (Pachyphytum × Echeveria). The '×' sign indicates that the plant is a hybrid. Sometimes the parents of a hybrid are not known, or the hybrid may have a complex ancestry. Many different forms can result from the same cross, and identification and naming are often difficult. For these reasons, the generic name may sometimes be followed directly by a fancy name, like Echinopsis 'Yascot' (p. 67) or simply by the word hybrid, as in Epiphyllum hybrids (p. 68).

In some cases a plant has two different names; these are

9

called synonyms. For a variety of reasons beyond the scope of this book, the names of some plants are changed from time to time. There is no doubt that considerable confusion exists in the nomenclature of cacti and other succulents. In the case of cacti, especially, it has frequently happened that certain genera have been divided into several smaller genera. One example is the genus Opuntia (prickly-pear), which has been divided into more than ten separate genera.

If you are a beginner I can well imagine that you are not all that interested in this matter of nomenclature. In any case a plant may have two names that can each be correct, depending on the classification used, in such a case it depends on one's personal preference or opinion which name is used. The choice of classification used is a matter for personal preference, and hence the name adapted.

In the nomenclature used in this book I have been guided, wherever possible, by the book *Flora of House and Greenhouse Plants* by Dr. B. K. Boom (1968). Dr. Boom is an authority on botanical nomenclature and has been involved in the setting up of international rules for the naming of cultivated plants.

THE ORIGIN, STRUCTURE AND ADAPTATION OF SUCCULENTS

Leaf cactus

Spherical and columnar shapes

It is widely believed that cacti originated in the tropical jungles of South America.

It is also thought that Pereskia, which has ordinary foliage, should be regarded as most like the progenitors of succulent cacti.

The succulent forms have adapted to changing climatic conditions, becoming tolerant to drought and capable of rapid water absorption. The moisture intake must take place within a short period, for when rain does fall in these dry regions, there is a fairly heavy downpour within a short time, but it soon disappears as a result of evaporation and very porous soil. Succulents must therefore be quick to get their share. Once they were able to do so (and it took them a long time to acquire this ability), they could conquer new territory, even regions where there is practically no rain at all—sometimes not a drop for an entire year.

The more cacti had to fall back on the more arid places, the more rapidly they lost their foliage. One of the functions of leaves is transpiration, and in cacti this must be restricted to a minimum. Cacti also have the capacity to store large amounts of water. A cactus body consists of up to 90 per cent of moisture and a great deal can be stored in the various shapes (for instance the spherical form). In many succulents the epidermis is extra thick; sometimes it is further covered in a wax layer or a dense tissue of hair. Succulents moreover possess few pores, and those they do have lie deep within the skin. All these measures taken by mother nature reduce evaporation to a minimum. As you see, everything is aimed at enabling the plants to survive in a barren environment. I might also mention an example which indicates the relative rate of water-loss in a hedgehog cactus and that in a foliage plant. It has been calculated that the rate of water-loss in this particular cactus is 6,000 times less.

There are also cacti and other succulents which withdraw into the ground during the dry season. This may, for instance, be the result of the root, anchored in the soil, shortening as it dries up, thus drawing the plant's body down.

The most striking behaviour is found in the so-called 'window-plants'. In these ultra-succulent plants e.g. Fenestraria only the tips of the leaves are visible above ground; these have 'windows' through which sunlight can enter, enabling photosynthesis to occur (this is a chemical process initially producing sugars). It is beyond the scope of this book to discuss the effect of these 'windows' in greater detail.

In Lithops species (Living stones) the old, shrivelled leaves (frequently there is only one pair) protect the young, newly developing pair of leaves.

Sometimes, in various cacti and other succulents, there are tuber-shaped roots capable of storing extra moisture. In order to provide the largest possible area of water absorption, cacti often have a widely branching shallow root system.

Not all cacti are spherical or columnar in shape. There are also forms (Opuntia) with flattened joints or pads; these have taken over the function of leaves. Many Opuntias in fact develop small leaves on their young shoots, but in most species they are soon shed.

Cacti which grow as epiphytes, lodging in the branches of trees, but taking no nourishment from them, and notably the so-called joint- and leaf-cacti, have a larger breathing surface and grow in entirely different (damper) conditions.

You will no doubt wonder how the numerous succulents that have dispensed with foliage feed themselves, since assimilation is one of a leaf's tasks. In the first place many succulents grow in countries where there is plenty of bright light, so that a much smaller assimilating surface will suffice. Since many cacti, as well as other succulents, have developed warts, or even ribs, the surface has in any case been enlarged to some extent. Pad cacti go a step further: here the flattened 'branches' are placed irregularly, one above the other. It is generally believed that the thorns (they should not really be called spines) serve to protect the plant from being eaten by animals. This would seem to be an acceptable theory, but on the other hand there are quite a few desert animals that eat cacti, thorns and all, the iguanas of the Galapagos Islands, to give an example.

A similar purpose is ascribed to the hairs covering certain plants; this is thought to be a protection against cold, or, on the other hand, against fierce sunlight. But in that case how do we explain the fact that cacti as bare as billiard balls are found in the mountains? And how do innumerable other succulents survive in South Africa without a covering of woolly hairs?

Succulents other than cacti are sometimes divided into leaf-

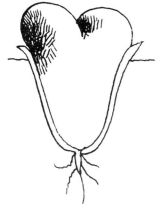

Window-plant

Pad cactus

and stem-succulents. In the former it is the leaves that are thick and sappy, in the second group only the stems. However, there are also species in which both stem(s) and foliage are succulent.

As we have seen, there are cacti without thorns, but there are also non-cactus succulents which do have fearsome armour (see Euphorbia grandicornis and Euphorbia pseudo-cactus). Cactus thorns vary greatly in form and strength. In some cases they are as much as 10 cm in length (as in for instance Stetsonia coryne), in others they are broad. Hooked thorns are found on certain Mammillaria, Ferocactus and other species; other cacti may only possess long, silvery hairs (Cephalocereus senilis). A few climbing cacti even use their thorns to cling to other plants; Pereskia aculeata is an example.

There is also considerable variation in the colours of the thorns; they may be pink, grey, black, brown, white or reddish in colour.

The most sensational feature of cacti as well as of numerous other succulents is the flowers. They occur in nearly all colours: only blue is lacking. There are even some with greenish or brownish flowers. They attract all kinds of insects, for instance bees, butterflies and moths, but also humming-birds, honey-birds and bats.

In some species the flowers are very large: diameters of 35 cm have been encountered, but miniature flowers also occur, in cacti as well as in innumerable other succulents. As a rule cactus flowers grow singly; they may appear near the growing point as well as from parts of the plant that have developed earlier.

Extra growth of woolly hairs or thorns frequently heralds the appearance of flowers. Some cacti develop a so-called cephalium; this is particularly obvious in Melocactus species. The cephalium is a kind of cap consisting of woolly hairs and thorns from which the flowers appear.

The ultimate purpose of flowering is the production of seed. Here, too, the maintenance of the species is of the greatest importance. The seeds are contained in fruits varying considerably in shape and colour. Many cactus fruits are edible. Birds, too, eat them and thus assist in the distribution of seed, as do ants.

Seeds are as varying in shape, colour and size, as the cacti themselves. Germination may take from a week to several

Rosette shape

13

months. In certain spurges (Euphorbia) the seed is forcibly expelled, while the seeds of many Stapelia species possess a feathery plume which helps to disperse the seeds more widely.

I hope the above will give you some idea of the variations which exists in the world of succulents. The best example of all is, perhaps, the size the plants may reach. Some cacti (e.g. Carnegiea) may grow to 20–25 m and a number of Euphorbia species become sizeable trees. On the other hand there are miniature cacti and other succulents, such as Rebutia minuscula and Lithops.

THE GEOGRAPHICAL DISTRIBUTION OF CACTI

All cacti belong to one botanical family, the Cactaceae. In nearly all members of this family the name is apt, for the Greek word kaktos means thistle. It is believed that cacti originated chiefly in South America, but they now occur in an area stretching from Patagonia (at a latitude of 50°S) to Canada (latitude of 52°N). While it might be thought that cacti occur mainly in tropical and subtropical regions, this enormous area of distribution tells us otherwise: they occur also in cold regions, even in places where it may freeze in winter. Many species grow at high altitudes; some even occur on the snowline. However, it is in Mexico, and in Peru, Bolivia and Argentina that the greatest concentration of cacti is indeed found. Mexico is always regarded as the cactus country *par excellence*, the more so as it is known that it was from this country that cacti were first brought to Europe. Moreover, the earliest known descriptions of cacti concern species occurring there. The cactus is even represented in the Mexican coat of arms. It is believed that more than 700 species grow in that country. Numerous Mammillaria, Coryphantha, Astrophytum and Echinofossulocactus species have their native habitat in Mexico. And not only cacti, but also species of Sedum, Echeveria and Agave are 'at home' there. Some species also occur further north, e.g. in California. A very well-known species (made popular also by the many cartoons in which it appears) is Carnegiea gigantea, a columnar cactus shaped like a candelabrum; this occurs in Arizona. Another North American cactus area which should be mentioned is Texas. Further east the population decreases and the few cacti which have penetrated the north are mainly Opuntia species.

In general it may be said that cacti originating in the U.S.A. are more difficult to grow in our part of the world than their cousins from the plateaux of Mexico and South America, where the rainfall is a little higher and average temperatures cooler. Our long, dark and damp winters, together with frequently damp and cool summers, are not exactly what the cacti from the semi-deserts of North- and Central American cacti are used to.

The rising popularity of South American cacti in Europe is of a fairly recent phenomenon, mainly due to the explorations of various energetic field collectors.

In South America it is the north-western part of Argentina and Bolivia which yield the greatest riches in cacti. It is here that Lobivia, Rebutia, Parodia and Echinopsis have their native habitat. Peru has also become important, especially in recent years as the source of such genera as Espostoa and Oroya.

Cacti may in any case be found in practically all the other South American countries, including Chile, Uruguay, Paraguay, Brazil, Ecuador, Colombia and Venezuela. Many epiphytic leaf-cacti are found in the forests of Brazil, including Rhipsalidopsis, Rhipsalis and Schlumbergera. The statement that all cacti are of American origin (including the Opuntia species introduced to Australia and South Africa and southern Europe) is contradicted by a single genus only: a few Rhipsalis species occur in Africa and Madagascar, and may possibly be native there. However, there is a school of thought which holds that their presence in Africa is the result of distribution by birds, and that the species originated on the continent of America.

THE GEOGRAPHICAL DISTRIBUTION OF OTHER SUCCULENTS

As we have seen, cacti originate almost without exception in America. The other succulents have a much wider area of distribution. They occur in all continents and are found in all those places where nature makes it difficult for plants to survive and forces them to store up reserves. They therefore even occur high in the mountains, near the polar regions, and in other places where they can enjoy rain for brief periods only. Nevertheless their greatest concentration is found in the semi-desert regions of America, Africa and Asia.

South Africa provides a particularly wide area of succulent distribution. Well-known genera, such as Lithops, Argyroderma, Gasteria, Faucaria, Aloe and Haworthia occur there. Others, such as Euphorbia, also occur, but—chiefly because the genera in question include so many species—their area of distribution is much greater.

In this connection we should also mention the Canary Islands and the Cape Verde Islands, where the Aeonium species, and other members of the Crassula family, occur in particularly large numbers.

It is incorrect to assume that Agave, Aloe and genera of the Mesembyranthemum group, so often found on the Riviera, etc., are natives of those regions. They have all been introduced there, subsequently running wild.

Many succulents not belonging to the Cactus family also occur in North America and especially in Mexico: Sedum morganianum, Sedum stahlii, Echeveria, Pachyphytum and Agave, to mention but a few of the most important.

In Europe the 'other' succulents are represented chiefly by hardy species of Sedum and Sempervivum: Sedum by numerous species of which about a dozen occur in Britain, and Sempervivum mainly in the mountains, e.g. in the Alps and the Pyrenees.

Asia, too, makes its contribution, for instance in the shape of some Euphorbiaceae (Spurge family), a number of Asclepiadaceae (Milkweed family) and Sedum species such as Sedum lineare, S. spectabile, S. lydium, S. cauticolum and S. sieboldii.

Australia is the native habitat of the genus Hoya.

THE CARE OF SUCCULENTS

In their native habitat many cacti and other succulents grow in a dry and sunny climate. Naturally it is impossible to imitate these conditions to perfection in our greenhouses or living-rooms. The main disadvantage is the lack of light in our long winters. Nevertheless years of experience have made it possible to cultivate successfully even the most difficult species.

It must be borne in mind that succulents do not all live in exactly the same natural conditions and that they should therefore not all be treated in the same way. The only aspect easily varied in practice is the water supply, but it would be a great mistake to consider this the sole factor.

A small greenhouse (see p. 36) in a sunny garden provides the most ideal environment, especially if it is heated in winter, but south- or south-east-facing windows are also very suitable. On sunny balconies the plants may be grown for prolonged periods in cold frames or balcony propagators.

Window-greenhouse

I even know a cactus collector who cultivates 9,000 specimens in a shed of which the roof has been replaced by glass; this is, in fact, the largest private collection I have ever seen. Two of this man's sayings are: 'Once you have caught the cactus bug you'll never get rid of it' and 'A cactus is an undemanding plant. It almost seems to ask to be neglected. But neglect it with care.'

If you are not the fortunate owner of a greenhouse, a glazed shed-roof or a south- or south-east-facing window, your choice will necessarily be restricted. Many leaf cacti, Aloe, Haworthia, Gasteria, Sansevieria, Kalanchoe and a few others are satisfied with less, but good light is a prerequisite for all succulents.

It is a well-known fact that many cactus species like to be kept cool and dry in winter. At that time they should therefore not remain in the living-room. A bedroom with little or no heating is ideal in that period, but make sure the plants get plenty of light and cannot freeze. It must be possible to maintain a minimum temperature of 5 °C. Not all succulents are able to spend the winter in a practically unheated room — see the descriptions of the various plants in the alphabetical section of this book.

In summer a large number of species may be placed out of

doors, for instance, many Sedum and Crassula species, Agave, Aeonium, Echeveria, Rochea, Opuntia, Rebutia, Austrocylindropuntia and most of the so-called shrubby Mesembryanthemums. Needless to say cold, damp summers (such as in 1974) provide less favourable outdoor conditions for succulents, and smaller species are ideally grown in a cold frame, so that, when the weather gods are not propitious, the plants may be put under glass.

Most succulents are now cultivated in plastic pots. Occasionally they are grown in tins, but these have the disadvantage that they rust and cannot be stacked when empty. Among plastic pots I consider the square varieties more suitable. They are obtainable in several sizes and can be placed close together, thus making the best use of the available space. Ordinary clay pots are now rarely used by cactus collectors. The belief that pots should be able to 'breathe' has been relegated to the land of myths. Actually I think that stone pots are more attractive, but roots often become attached to the sides, which hampers re-potting. In plastic pots the soil temperature is, moreover, slightly higher and this encourages growth. Plants grown in plastic pots should be given slightly less water, since no water evaporates through the sides.

On the question of what compost to use there is marked divergence of opinion among cactus growers. Many of them prefer special mixtures. Proprietary cactus mixtures are also available.

Ordinary loam-based potting compost, sold in small as well as in large packs, may be used, preferably mixed with a one-third part of river sand. The addition of some clay and, if available, a little wood-ash, is also recommended. These contain innumerable minerals which encourage growth and improve the colour of the thorns. The modern soilless composts, containing peat, sand and base fertilizer also give very satisfactory results.

It is most important that the soil should contain little or no lime, since most succulents are lime-haters.

Not too high a pH (degree of alkalinity) is essential.

In compost with loam, most cacti require very little fertilizer. Provided the plants are regularly repotted, and a little base fertilizer is added to the soil, additional feeding is rarely necessary. When you nevertheless decide that the plants deserve a little extra, or you are using soilless compost in which the nutrients are soon exhausted, use one of the special cactus fertilizers which are available. Do not use an ordinary proprietary plant food in which the nitrogen content will be too high and the phosphate content too low.

Epiphytic cacti (Epiphyllum, etc.) and various succulents not belonging to the cactus family, may, however, be fed with the same fertilizer as ordinary pot plants.

The plants are given a feed only in the growing season, preferably at the beginning of this period.

Correct watering is without any doubt the greatest problem in the cultivation of succulents. It is difficult to lay down fixed rules, but most cactus growers are of the opinion that an occasional generous soak is better than a little water every day. The correct amount depends on the size of the plant, the species, its position, the temperature and the time of the year. It should further be borne in mind that most succulents require relatively large amounts of water in the growing season; the water supply should gradually be increased from the beginning of this period onwards. Once the plants have started into growth, spray-misting may be very beneficial. Here, too, experience will prove to be the best teacher.

Always make sure that by the evening the plants are dry again. The water should be as lime-free as possible (in other words, use rain-water in preference to tap-water) and should be at room- or greenhouse temperature.

It is not advisable to water in bad weather. Most species should be kept practically dry in winter.

The best time for repotting is just before the start of the growing season. As a rule the removal of the soil-ball presents no problem; only cacti grown in clay pots occasionally stick to the sides. In this case it may be necessary to break the pot to avoid damage to the roots.

In clay pots a few crocks in the bottom of the pot improve drainage and stop the soil falling out.

Always repot plants at their original depth. Freshly repotted specimens require extra care with watering.

MONTH BY MONTH CARE OF SUCCULENTS

It is no simple matter to record the care needed by succulents from month to month. All manner of circumstances, often varying from one plant to another, play a part. The calendar that follows should therefore be regarded merely as a general guideline.

JANUARY

For the sake of their health the large majority of succulents require a rest in this month. Watering is hardly, if at all, necessary. Certainly the plants do not need to grow in this period. However, in clear, sunny weather occasional mist-spraying is desirable to create a slightly humid atmosphere, though the plants must not actually get wet. If watering should prove to be necessary (once a month for instance), the water should, where the pots are plunged, be poured on to the surrounding peat and not on the pot-soil. Most young seedlings should just be kept in growth and must not be allowed to dry out.

This advice applies chiefly to species which must be kept very cool in winter. Those that are kept at slightly higher temperatures must be given a little water once a fortnight. If you grow your plants in a greenhouse, it will do no harm in good weather to ventilate for an hour or so at midday, provided the outside temperature is above 5°C. All plants appreciate fresh air.

Epiphytic cacti, such as Epiphyllum, etc., should regularly be given a little water. They differ to a considerable degree from their relatives.

FEBRUARY

In this month, too, rest is of the essence, though in a few groups, such as Mammillaria and Rebutia, flower buds may start to form if the weather is favourable. The plants hesitantly start into growth, which means that they may very carefully be given a little water. Leaf cacti, such as Epiphyllum must now also regularly be given a little water. Repotting may now commence, but be careful to preserve the soil-ball and not to damage the roots.

It is essential to check for red spider, which may occur particularly if the atmosphere is dry and the temperature increases.

Prevent your succulents drying out entirely: keep a careful check. Spray-misting, as described under 'January', is again desirable. Ventilate the greenhouse in mild weather.

MARCH

Most succulents are starting into growth and all necessary repotting may be undertaken. Always use a proprietary cactus compost or a mixture such as described on p. 19. Plants which flower early, e.g. Rebutia, certain Echinocereus species and Epiphyllum, are best repotted after flowering.

Provided the weather outside is good leaf-succulents not belonging to the cactus family must now be watered regularly. Other succulents, too, will be grateful for a weekly shower with the finest possible spray. However, for Living stones and similar plants the rule remains valid: little or no water; only just enough to keep the roots alive.

Sowing may now commence, but if you are a beginner you would do better to wait another month. Bottom heat is of the greatest importance when sowing cacti and other succulents.

Incidentally, it may already be necessary in this month to provide light shading against bright sunlight, for the plants are not yet used to intensive light, and, of course, do not forget to provide ventilation.

APRIL

Growth has now commenced in earnest. This means that, contrary to what is often believed, we need no longer be so sparing with the water supply. Try to water in the morning and use water (preferably rain water) at room- or greenhouse temperature. Lithops species should as yet be left alone: they are still dormant.

If you have not yet repotted it's high time to do so. Ample ventilation and humidity are absolutely essential in an unshaded greenhouse, since otherwise the plants are bound to be damaged. Better to avoid any risk and provide shading.

Sowing may now be undertaken in many places and propagation from cuttings can also commence.

The majority of plants require a fair amount of water from now on. It is practically impossible to indicate the correct amounts, for all kinds of factors, such as temperature and atmospheric humidity, play a part.

MAY–JUNE
Quite a few succulents prefer to spend the summer out of doors. One of these is the Agave, but there are numerous others. The move should take place in the second half of May, when the risk of night frost is minimal. It is best to plant them out, but it is also possible to put them in the garden or on the balcony in their pots.

Greenhouses must now be thoroughly ventilated in warm sunny weather and when the air is dry.

JULY
Summer is the time to give the plants special cactus food. Plenty of light, a fair amount of water and nourishment, encourage favourable development. Lithops, Conophytum and similar species are now also watered; the amount need not be all that much less than that given to other non-cactus succulents. Old leaves which have shrivelled up may be removed, for these form ideal breeding ground for mealy bug.

Many species may still be grafted or grown from cuttings. Epiphyllum species appreciate a dose of organic fertilizer.

AUGUST
In very bright sunlight ample ventilation is essential and shading may be necessary, but this does not mean that the plants should not be placed in the best available light.

Succulents originating in South Africa now enjoy a period of most vigorous growth. Lithops and Conophytum species should be watered fairly freely.

Seedlings of cacti sown early in the year and large enough to handle, may be pricked out. Be careful not to damage the root system and make sure they continue growing.

The plants may now be given their last feed: in September this is usually discontinued. When the weather is dull and close, watering should be restricted to a minimum. There is serious risk of an attack by red spider, especially if conditions are hot and dry. If necessary spray with a proprietary insecticide. Avoid damage to the plants.

SEPTEMBER
The growing season is coming to an end and we must start to

prepare the plant for the coming darker and cooler period. This process is called 'hardening off': ventilation is still essential, but draughts must be avoided as much as possible.

Gradually decrease the water supply. This does not apply to most leaf-succulents, Lithops and related species.

Most of the plants which have spent the summer outside should now gradually be brought indoors. Agave and a few other very hardy species may continue to enjoy the fresh air a little longer.

OCTOBER

Any shading of the greenhouse should be removed, for all available light is now welcome. The water supply should be drastically diminished; only Lithops and similar species may still be given a little.

It is also important to continue to ventilate. This may be done even at night, provided the temperature does not drop below 10°C.

Cacti and other succulents may remain in the cold frame until the end of the month, as long as it is not too damp. Agaves should now be brought under cover.

NOVEMBER

Epiphyllum enters its dormant season; the water supply should be drastically, but gradually, reduced. Feeding would be harmful.

(Nearly) all cacti and other succulents should be placed in a cool room (10°C) in the best available light.

It is essential to keep them dry; only young seedlings and recently grafted cacti may be watered sparingly. Where it is necessary to keep plants in the living-room, they should be placed as close to the window as possible and watered sparingly.

DECEMBER

The year is coming to an end and our favourite plants are resting. Only a well cared for Schlumbergera may be allowed to justify its popular name 'Christmas cactus'. Let this flowering beauty convince you of the fact that better times, times of growth and flowering, are coming for all other cacti and succulents.

THE PROPAGATION OF SUCCULENTS

Once you 'get the feel' of the cultivation of succulents, you might like to venture upon their propagation.

There are three possible methods, viz. seed-raising, growing from cuttings, and grafting, although properly speaking the latter is not primarily a method of propagation.

Seed-raising is probably the most rewarding procedure for a collector. Patience is of the essence, for you must not expect them to get off the mark as fast as, say, African marigolds, snapdragons or lupins.

There is something adventurous in growing plants from seed. We are attracted by the unknown and the final result is always fascinating. One advantage is the fact that plants grown from seed are accustomed 'from the cradle' to the prevailing climatic conditions, for as a rule they will spend the rest of their lives in the same environment.

The seeds of succulent plants germinate in greatly varying circumstances. This is readily understood, for as we have seen they originate in many different places. Nevertheless the large majority of seeds will germinate satisfactorily at a temperature of between 20 and 25 °C (68–77 °F).

Sowing is best done in the period March–May if the temperature is adequate and there is plenty of light. It is possible to sow earlier, but in that case special steps must be taken: the temperature of the seed compost must be increased and additional light must be provided by artificial means.

The sowing medium must be porous, limefree, sterile and moisture-retaining. Proprietary cactus compost meets these requirements. It can be bought in garden shops in small packs. The soil is preferably put in new, shallow trays of some man-made material (e.g. hard plastic or polystyrene), and is then pressed down gently with a piece of wood or a matchbox. When sowing very fine seed it is advisable to sieve the top layer to a very fine tilth.

The seeds are now distributed as evenly as possible and again pressed down carefully. The seed tray is then covered with a glass pane. It is important to maintain an even temperature and degree of humidity. Until germination occurs the sowing medium must be kept moist. Temporary shading against bright sunlight may be provided by a newspaper. In favourable conditions some seeds may germinate within a week, but others will take several months.

The seedlings must be regularly inspected. If a lot of condensation occurs on the glass, the pane should be turned over. It is essential to admit a little air from time to time. Once the seedlings have developed satisfactorily, the glass is removed.

For the first year of their lives the seedlings can remain in the seed tray unless becoming crowded, but they should be pricked out not later than the spring of their second year into another tray with fresh soil, or to separate pots, depending on their size.

Most Opuntia and Cereus species, Gymnocalycium, Mammillaria, Notocactus, some Kalanchoe strains and many species of Haworthia, Sedum and other Crassulaceae are easily grown from seed.

A large number of succulent plants may successfully be propagated from cuttings. Many of them produce side shoots which are easily detached from the mother plant (e.g. Mammillaria, Echinopsis, Gasteria and Haworthia). Sometimes the plant is encouraged to form shoots by removing or damaging the growing point.

Species with long stems are very easily propagated. The stems are cut up into sections; these are left to dry a little and are then rooted in a sandy mixture. The flat joints of Opuntia species also strike readily. Sedum species, Rochea, Hoya, Euphorbia milii, Delosperma, Oscularia and many others may be grown from shoots.

The great advantage of vegetative propagation is that the young plants will have exactly the same characteristics as the parent plant. Hybrids cannot usually be perpetuated from seed, because the offspring would possess a mixture of features inherited from the different parents. It is for this reason that some popular varieties of Epiphyllum, Rhipsalidopsis, Schlumbergera and a few succulents other than cacti are increased solely by the vegetative method.

The best time for taking cuttings is in June–July, i.e. in the middle of the growing season. An even temperature and a dry environment are important to encourage the wounds to dry and to promote root formation.

Some succulents, such as Bryophyllum (= Kalanchoe) develop young plants along the margin or at the tip of their

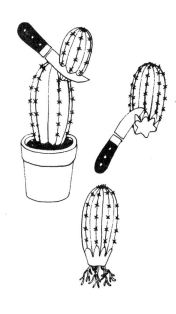

Propagation from cuttings

Grafting

leaves. Sansevieria and a few other succulents may be increased by division.

Grafting is a method used, among other reasons, to quicken the growth and flowering of the weaker species; this applies particularly to cacti.

Species with a very delicate root system are also better cultivated on a stock with stronger roots, since otherwise, for instance, they may not withstand the winter well. Also, the popular red, pink, violet, orange, yellow and brown Gymnocalycium strains, which assimilate weakly, if at all, are dependent on green stock. Cristate forms are also frequently grafted, since otherwise they are liable not to survive.

The following are some of the species suitable as stock for grafting: Cereus peruvianus, Cereus jamacaru, Trichocereus spachianus, Eriocereus jusbertii, Pereskia aculeata, Pereskiopsis spathulata and Hylocereus guatemalense.

Spring and summer are the best grafting seasons; at this time the chance of success is greatest.

Straight cut grafting is the method used for many cacti. In this method both stock and scion are cut straight across with a sharp knife. The edges of the stock are trimmed obliquely and the two sections are joined. All this must be done as quickly as possible. To encourage union and to prevent the scion falling off, the whole thing is held together by one or two rubber bands. Union will take place within a few days and the rubber bands can be removed after a week or two.

In the case of Christmas cacti and other flat-jointed species, the cleft method is used. A cut is made down the stock; the scion is trimmed into a wedge-shape and inserted in the cleft. Secure with a cactus thorn or with a clothes peg.

There are various other methods, but these are beyond the scope of this book.

When grafting, perfect cleanliness is always of the greatest importance.

CRISTATE FORMATION IN CACTI AND OTHER SUCCULENTS

Crest- or cristate form

The word 'monstrosity' (malformation or abnormality) covers a large number of deviations in plant growth.

Flowers which have a larger number of petals than is normal (i.e. are double-flowered) should actually also be classified among the 'monstrosities', as should foliage variegation and abnormal flower formation.

Fasciation (flattened stems) is a particular form of monstrosity. It occurs in the stems of a variety of plants; in some cases the deviation is specially cultivated. Fasciated forms are known of certain willows, conifers and Sedums. It is not known with absolute certainty in what conditions abnormalities will develop, but it is a striking fact that in some plants (e.g. dandelion) deviations occur regularly, in others rarely if ever.

Cristate (or crested) and monstrose forms also occur in cacti and other succulents, these, too, are 'monstrosities'.

Cristate cacti have a large number of growing points instead of only one. These grow together in one plane, like a comb. Cristate forms are known of Opuntia vestita, Cereus jamacaru, Lobivia pentlandii, Rebutia minuscula, Lophophora williamsii and others, and among other succulents, of Echeveria agavoides. Seed collected from cristate forms very rarely produces specimens with similar deviation. In any case cristate forms do not often flower. They are also difficult to grow from cuttings and as a rule grafting on vigorous stock is the only way to perpetuate them. In other words, the part of the cactus which has grown into a crest is divided and the sections are grafted on stock of another species. The monstrose or 'rock forms' are closely related to the crest forms. The best known among them is Cereus peruvianus 'Monstruosus'. This form has irregularly deformed stems with unusually shaped ribs and short brown thorns. It is a remarkable fact that its seed always produces at least a few specimens with the same characteristics.

Large and varied collections often contain quite a few of these freak forms. Sometimes they are a collector's pride and joy.

SUCCULENTS AS PLANTS OF ECONOMIC VALUE

In this part of the world we enjoy cacti and other succulents for their beauty. We cultivate them with care in our greenhouses, living-rooms and gardens and frequently our efforts are crowned with success. However, in other countries they grow wild and in some regions they are used for entirely different purposes.

In developing countries such as Mexico, etc., the fruits of certain cacti, especially Opuntia, are used as food. In Mexico Opuntia fruits are called tunas, and are of great commercial importance. They are collected in their wild habitat, but are also harvested in specially cultivated plantations. They are greatly in demand, particularly in periods of drought, when other crops have failed. They may be eaten uncooked, but are also preserved in syrup and are even turned into an alcoholic drink called colonche. The drink does not keep well and is only made for private consumption. Tunas are also dried, first having been peeled.

It is certain that in the course of centuries Opuntia species and other cacti have saved many people, especially the indigenous Amerindians from death by starvation or thirst. These species, with little or no spine formation, also make excellent cattle fodder.

The edible fruits of Cereus plants are called pithaya. Edible fruits are also produced by Pereskia aculeata; they are rather like gooseberries.

Opuntia has been of importance in another respect as well, for it made an excellent breeding ground for the cochineal insect. The Amerindians made a carmine red dye from the insect even before the discovery of America by Columbus. The Spaniards later adopted this method, drying and grinding the insects, and using the dye to colour wool and silk. In modern times the advent of industrial chemical dye superseded the old practice.

Lophophora williamsii

A drug is made from Lophophora williamsii, a cactus without thorns that occurs in northern and central Mexico. The drug, peyotl, is a narcotic which causes hallucinations. It is still used and worshipped in Indian festivities lasting for days. Apparently peyotl is still being used in parts of Mexico.

Other cacti also contain alkaloids, and some have formerly been used in the treatment of heart conditions.

When studying the literature on the subject we find that succulents other than cacti also have unexpected properties. The best known example is sisal, made from the tough fibres of Agave sisalana leaves. The fibres of other Agave species, shorter and thicker in structure, are used in the manufacture of brushes. Yet another Agave, viz. A. salmiana, produces a drink called pulque. It does not keep, but is said to have a very pleasant taste. Some native tribes use the Agave juice for making mescal or tequila, a distilled spirit. The milky white liquid found in some Euphorbia species is highly poisonous; this was why African natives used to dip their arrow tips in it.

The lower part of many large cactus species turns woody in the course of time and the wood is used for a number of purposes, including the making of furniture.

The edges of the frayed leaves of certain Yucca species provide the material for making mats.

Needless to say, certain cacti may form a practically impenetrable hedge to keep out undesirable intruders. This then is the modest, but important role of succulents as economic plants. Even more important is the fact that they are capable of surviving in arid regions, where they relieve the almost unbearable climate by their mere presence. They provide a little shade and a modicum of dew. A little of their moisture evaporates and they furnish a minimal trace of humus in the soil, thus possibly giving other pertinacious plants a chance.

We can only guess at their commercial value in Europe, but the pleasure they give to collectors cannot be expressed in figures: it is inestimable.

PESTS AND DISEASES

The plant does not exist that is not threatened by some parasite or another. Succulents are no exception and in spite of all the good care we give them, our favourites may yet be attacked by parasites such as mealy bug, red spider, grubs, Phytophthora, Rhizoctonia, etc. Let me begin by establishing that plants grown in the best possible conditions are least prone to infection. This applies particularly to diseases such as mould and bacteria. The best possible conditions we can provide are adequate light, the correct temperature and relative degree of humidity, good soil and the correct proportion of nutrients. As with all plants, proper care is the best insurance against disease.

In addition to pests and fungi, yellow and red discoloration may occur; the cause is nearly always a physiological one. Yellowing may indicate excess watering or bad soil. Other causes may be: too low a temperature, weak roots or inadequate nourishment. The plants may be cured by taking them from their pots, removing bad roots and repotting in better soil. Red discoloration is frequently due to over-bright sunlight, particularly where the root system is not healthy, since this, too, will result in lack of moisture.

Cork formation occurs fairly often, especially in cacti; again there may be a mixture of causes. A combination of a relatively high atmospheric humidity, excessively moist soil and a low temperature has an extremely adverse effect and encourages the disease. Other culprits are: cold, hard (i.e. chalky) water and irregular watering.

Fungus diseases may cause rotting of the entire plant or of the base only (root rot). In general it may be said that too damp, too dark, too warm conditions and lack of ventilation increase the risk of an attack. There is little one can actually do. The soil must always be pure, in other words, fresh or sterilised. Always use new or disinfected pots. Affected plants are not easily saved. If caught in time, spraying with fungicides may help, but these remedies are not always readily available to the amateur. Diseased specimens should therefore be thrown away, or at any rate isolated from other plants.

Excellent remedies are available to combat aphids. Personally I prefer brands containing controls of plant-origin such as nicotine, pyrethrum and derris.

Mealy bugs are a widespread pest of succulent plants These tiny wax-covered insects suck the plant sap. They can be combated with methylated spirits, applied to the insects by means of a small brush. They must be removed or destroyed, as they multiply rapidly and can soon do serious damage. It's a laborious, but effective, method. Scale insects may be controlled in the same way, but in this case the scales should be brushed off before the liquid is applied. Most collectors nowadays use systemic insecticides, but these are not recommended for domestic use as they, and their fumes, are poisonous to humans also. The problem is that mature insects (females only) are covered by shields and these also cover the eggs and very young insects which later migrate to other parts of the plant; they can be attacked on the move.

Red spider can be a real pest, the more so as they form a very fine web. Spraying with insecticide is the best remedy. It is essential to repeat the treatment several times, for the eggs are not killed. Red spider thrives in a low degree of atmospheric humidity and fairly high temperatures: this should be borne in mind. In the case of other plants (roses, for instance) insects can be washed off by means of heavy hosing, but few succulents would tolerate this treatment.

About the worst that can happen to a cactus collector is an attack by root mealy bug. These woolly white lice, closely allied to the species which attacks stems and foliage, live on the roots and the base of the plants. They occur especially when the plants are (or must be) kept dry. Systemic insecticides are again the most effective remedy. Alternatively, one can shake off all the soil and to rinse the roots until no insects seem to be left. The roots are then dipped in methylated spirits and rinsed again. Re-pot in fresh cactus compost and keep the plants in quarantine for the time being.

Sow-bugs attacking young shoots may be captured in hollowed potatoes placed close to the plants.

Slugs and snails are controlled by special remedies available for the purpose.

Part of the succulent collection of the Horticultural Institute at Wageningen, The Netherlands.

SUITABLE PLANTS FOR BEGINNERS

When embarking upon a new hobby it is important to make a successful start. Disappointment in the early stages has led many an enthusiastic beginner to give up. I would therefore advise you to start with easy plants, that is, those that are guaranteed to be successful. This will not be difficult: there is a large choice of succulents that present few problems. As far as cacti are concerned, you would do best to select species of the genera Lobivia, Rebutia, Echinopsis, Notocactus, Gymnocalycium and Hamatocactus. Many Cereus and Mammillaria species and practically all Opuntia pad-cacti, are excellent for a beginner's collection. Leaf-cacti and those with flattened joints are also fairly easy to grow.

Among thornless succulents the following species may be recommended: Ceropegia, Crassula, Echeveria, Sedum, Kalanchoe (incl. Bryophyllum), Aloe, Haworthia, Gasteria, many Euphorbia species, Agave, Sansevieria, Senecio, Rochea, Oscularia, Lampranthus and Delosperma.

Once you have some experience you may successfully grow Conophytum, Pleiospilos and especially Lithops in a sunny living-room.

As you see, even a beginner can build up quite a collection, and when you've got your hand in you can go a step further and take on difficult customers such as Pelecyphora, Melocactus, Lophophora and many others.

Notocactus haselbergii, leninghausii and Chamaecereus silvestrii 'Cristate' combined in a pottery bowl.

WHERE TO BUY YOUR CACTI AND OTHER SUCCULENTS

A beginner starting a collection will have to buy plants from garden centres and florists, where there is often a considerable choice. Succulents are also frequently available from market stalls; some of these actually specialise.

Private collectors can also purchase plants from specialist cactus growers and may thus add rarer species to their collections.

A more advanced collector will be able to spread his nets a little wider by swopping with fellow-collectors. Membership of a cactus society is a great advantage.

GREENHOUSES

I am convinced—and can prove it with numerous examples—that in the cultivation of cacti and other succulents the best results are achieved by growing them in a greenhouse, where the maximum amount of light is available and where temperature and degree of humidity can be controlled. In the living-room this is, of course, not possible, for here we are chiefly concerned with our own comfort, while plants take a back seat. This does not mean that we cannot look after them to the best of our ability, and it is a well-known fact that many cacti and other succulents will thrive indoors.

But I repeat: in a greenhouse the results will undoubtedly be better, since here the conditions are, or at least can easily be made, more favourable.

Modern greenhouses are now practically always made of impregnated deal, Western Red Cedar and Redwood, and,

Above left: *young cactus seedlings. Initially no spines are visible.* Above right: *in the course of time their true nature will become obvious.* Below left: *a grafted scion is kept in place by a rubber band (Gymnocalycium mihanovichii 'Orange').* Below right: *Grafted specimens of Gymnocalycium, practically lacking in chlorophyll, find their way to our living-rooms in tens of thousands.*

above all, of aluminium. Deal is the cheapest, but requires maintenance and is the least durable. Cedar and redwood greenhouses will last a long time and will need little or no maintenance. Aluminium greenhouses are becoming most popular. The material is very light in weight and requires no maintenance of any kind. It is self-protecting because a thin anti-corrosion layer protects it from the weather. Greenhouses are available in a variety of designs.

Lean-to greenhouses, formerly greatly in demand, are still available. In a small garden they are undoubtedly useful, provided you have a south-facing wall.

However, free-standing greenhouses are now the most popular. They should preferably be positioned facing east and west, to provide the maximum of light in the dark months of the year. No need to despair if the situation of your garden makes this impossible, for other positions are also acceptable.

Free-standing greenhouses are available with straight as well as with sloping sides; the former are used most frequently. They may be glazed all over, but in some designs the lower part of the sides is made of asbestos cement or wood. Though providing a saving in fuel costs, the latter makes it impossible to grow plants under the staging. I feel that an all-glass greenhouse is to be preferred for succulent collections. Experience has taught me that numerous species will do very well under the staging.

Of course greenhouses are available in varying widths, lengths and heights. The last is quite important: it must be possible to stand upright and work comfortably. Before you buy, make sure it is the right 'fit'. Very small greenhouses are available for balconies, etc.

If you are a handyman I recommend a greenhouse supplied in do-it-yourself kit-form; this will save you a considerable amount of money.

Staging is essential, especially if the cacti are to be planted out. Staging is frequently made of asbestos cement sheets placed on a galvanized iron or aluminium frame. Simple wooden tables may also be installed. Now that many cacti and other succulents are grown in plastic pots which need not be plunged in soil, the latter is a perfectly acceptable solution. If you add a few hanging pots, you can grow plants at three

Yucca aloifolia in a modern interior

levels and collect the largest possible number of species within a small space.

There are always pessimists who raise objections, but I well remember a visit to Mr. Atkinson, a cactus collector who lives in Tunbridge Wells, who showed me a collection of at least 500 species in a tiny aluminium greenhouse. He, too, grew them at three levels and the plants were in exceptionally good condition. In winter he maintained a minimum temperature of about 5°C.

This brings me to the problems concerning heating. The output of which your heating apparatus should be capable depends mainly on the cubic capacity of the greenhouse and on the minimum temperature required: 10°C should be aimed at. To avoid subsequent disappointment, get a correct estimate of the heating capacity of your apparatus. Various methods of heating can be used.

Electricity provides a particularly good, but expensive, form of heating. One solution is to have a radiator connected to the central heating system in your house; in that case the greenhouse must be situated close to the house.

Temperature control necessarily includes ventilation and shading. When purchasing a greenhouse, check that it can be adequately ventilated. If you can afford it, it is a good idea to fit automatic vent openers. With certain types of heaters the temperature can be exactly controlled by means of a thermostat.

It is also important to be able to shade the greenhouse. Various types of roller blinds, internal or external are available, and some kinds (internal) are suitable for small amateur greenhouses. Permanent methods such as greenhouse shading painted on the glass, are cheaper but cannot quickly be removed when more light is required. Textured glass is also effective; the light is diffused more evenly and there is no shadow. Once you become a really keen collector, you would be well advised to purchase a greenhouse.

A well-lit arrangement of a large number of cacti

IMPORTANT COLLECTIONS

When you have become interested in everything connected with succulent plants, it makes sense to visit fine collections. You will no doubt come into contact with other amateurs who have assembled beautiful collections, but various professional growers will also welcome a visit, even if you do not necessarily intend to buy. In most cases you should first make an appointment. Some growers have fine private collections in addition to their commercial section.

Notable collections associated with commercial enterprises are the Ashington Botanical Collection, Holly Gate Nurseries Ltd., Billingshurst Lane, Ashington, Sussex (admission 25p), and The Exotic Collection, 16 Franklin Road, Worthing, Sussex (admission by appointment only). There are also reference collections at Whitestone Gardens, Ltd., The Cactus Houses, Sutton-under-Whitestonecliffe, Thirsk, North York-shire, and at Abbey Brook Cactus Nursery, Old Hackney Lane, Matlock, Derbyshire.

Public collections to visit are those at the Royal Botanic Gardens at Kew, Richmond, Surrey, and the Royal Botanic Garden, at Edinburgh. The municipal authorities at some south-coast towns stage outdoor displays in summer, including Eastbourne and Paignton. The most extensive out-of-doors display in Britain, however, is at Tresco Abbey Gardens, Tresco, Isles of Scilly, Cornwall.

An imposing Espostoa melanostele in its natural environment (a side valley of the Eulalia Valley, Peru, 1.3.1969).

SOCIETIES

Cactus & Succulent Society of Great Britain
Membership Secretary: Mrs. R. Horan
23 Nimrod Road, London, S.W.16.

National Cactus & Succulent Society
Membership Secretary: Miss W. E. Dunn
43 Dewar Drive, Sheffield S7 2GR

African Succulent Plant Society
Honorary Secretary: K. Grantham
21 Wadhurst Avenue, Luton, Beds. LU3 1UP

There are several other societies based in Britain specializing in particular groups. They include The Mammillaria Society, The Sempervivum Society, The Chileans (S. American Cacti), The International Asclepiadaceae Society. All these publish illustrated bulletins, as do The Exotic Collection and Holly Gate Nurseries Ltd., mentioned under important collections.

Adromischus cooperi

Aeonium arboreum

ADROMISCHUS COOPERI

In very dry regions of South-West Africa and Namaqualand quite a number of Adromischus species are found. They are closely related to the genus Cotyledon. Most species form rosettes of thick, fleshy, often multicoloured leaves, but some develop short trunks. The fleshy leaves drop easily; they root quickly, thus forming new plants.

Adromischus cooperi has dark, reddish-brown blotches on the leaves. Adromischus trigynus, too, has irregularly shaped, chocolate-brown blotching. Plain green species also occur. The flowers are lilac or greenish in colour. These plants are grown in the same way as Cotyledon species.

AEONIUM ARBOREUM

Most of the approximately 40 species of Aeonium grow wild in the Canary Islands. The species illustrated is a native of Morocco, but has run wild in many other Mediterranean countries. It is a shrub with a woody stem, up to 1 m (3 feet) in height. The leaves grow in rosettes of up to 20 cm (8 in.) across. The lower leaves continually drop, leaving obvious scars, while new leaves constantly develop at the top. Brown-leaved strains such as 'Atropurpureum' and 'Zwartkop' are the ones most frequently cultivated. Aeonium species like nutritious, porous soil. The actual growing period occurs in winter and the plants should therefore be adequately watered in that season. From late May until mid-September they may be placed out of doors.

Agave americana 'Argenteovariegata'   *Agave filifera compacta*

AGAVE AMERICANA

Everyone will recognize this fine, decorative plant. Its native habitat is probably in Mexico, but this Agave has run wild in practically all (sub-) tropical regions and in addition has been grown in tubs since the late Middle Ages. In spite of the size which older plants may attain in the course of time, it is very suitable for use indoors. Give it a sunny and warm situation. Large specimens may be put outside in summer. In winter the temperature may drop to 5°C, but in that period the plant must be watered very sparingly. Young shoots growing from mature specimens can be detached and potted separately when they have reached 8–10 cm (3–4 in.). There are yellow- and white-edged strains as well as the blue-green species.

AGAVE FILIFERA

Agave filifera 'Compacta', a smaller growing Agave is a very attractive plant. As the specific name, meaning 'bearing threads', indicates, long threads grow from the leaves, which are up to 25 cm (10 in.) in length. Among other so-called dwarf species one of the choicest is Agave victoriae-reginae; this plant may nevertheless grow to quite a good size. Plants with a diameter of 50 cm (20 in.) or more are not exceptional. Its most striking features are the white, horny stripes and the dark brown spines. These species require the same care as Agave americana, but they are usually kept indoors throughout the year.

Aloe arborescens   *Aloe mitriformis*

ALOE ARBORESCENS

There are said to be as many as 100 Aloe species, all occurring in Africa. A number of very remarkable forms grow in Madagascar. Many species are also found growing on a large scale in Mediterranean countries, where they easily run wild.

Some Aloe species grow into trees up to 10 m (33 feet) in height, for instance Aloe pillansii, but dwarf species only a few centimetres tall also occur.

A very well-known species is Aloe arborescens, often used as a house plant. Cuttings pass from hand to hand and the plant has thus become widely distributed. At one time its sap was used as an anodyne to burns. Pot-grown Aloe arborescens plants rarely flower, but planted out in a greenhouse they may produce fine red blooms.

ALOE MITRIFORMIS

The cultivation of this and other Aloe species present practically no problems. Clayey soil mixed with some leaf-mould is the most suitable medium. In summer they may be placed out of doors and must be watered fairly generously. Water sparingly in winter. Be careful never to pour water into the centre of the rosettes.

In addition to the Aloe mitriformis illustrated, which has clear red flowers, I should like to draw your attention to Aloe aristata. This plant forms small rosettes which close up into a ball if kept very dry. When more water is given the rosettes will rapidly open. A very suitable form for indoor cultivation is Aloe variegata, sometimes called the Partridge-breasted aloe. Its leaves are beautifully marked with dark and creamy transverse bands.

47

Anacampseros rufescens   *Aporocactus flagelliformis*

ANACAMPSEROS RUFESCENS

The family Portulacaceae is represented in this book by the genus Anacampseros. This interesting genus of stem- and leaf-succulents is difficult both to obtain and to grow and as a rule is found only in large collections.

The species illustrated is a leaf-succulent. The lilac-pink flowers appear on fairly long stalks and quickly fade. Certain Anacampseros species, such as Anacampseros papyracea, have protective colouring. The white stems, covered in numerous bracts, attract little attention in the quartz lands which are their usual habitat.

Anacampseros species require porous soil. Water sparingly in summer and withhold water in winter.

APOROCACTUS FLAGELLIFORMIS (Rat's Tail Cactus) .

The Rat's Tail catcus is frequently found in the windowsills of farmhouses, especially in Switzerland. It is one of the few hanging cacti. In favourable conditions the tail-like stems may grow to as much as a metre long ($3\frac{1}{4}$ feet).

This is an excellent cactus for a beginner. Properly cared for the plant will flower profusely in spring; the flowers are fairly large and deep pink in colour. To achieve an abundance of flowers it is necessary to grow the plant in a good light. A dormant season in a cool situation is essential; during this time the plant must not be kept entirely dry. From mid-February onwards it should be moved to a warmer spot in full sun.

During the flowering and growing seasons it requires a fair amount of water.

Aptenia cordifolia 'Variegata'

Argyroderma speciosum

APTENIA CORDIFOLIA

Ice plants (Cryophytum cristallinum), frequently grown in warm, sunny spots in the garden, often flower profusely.

The large pastel-coloured flowers are very eye-catching and are always much appreciated. A close relation, sometimes called Mesembryanthemum, is this Aptenia cordifolia, which has very small flowers (about 1.5 cm ($\frac{1}{2}$ in.) across), invariably rose-pink in colour.

Like the ice plant, this species originates in South Africa. The plain green species is rarely seen; the variegated form with even smaller flowers occurs more often. At one time the plant was occasionally used as a bedding plant (for instance in mosaic planting), and you might therefore try to grow some in a sunny spot out of doors.

ARGYRODERMA SPECIOSUM

It is very difficult to distinguish the various species belonging to the genus Argyroderma. Even among specialists there is divergence of opinion.

All the species originate in a small area, the so-called Plain of Kners in Little Namaqualand. They are true quartz-loving plants and will grow best in a very sandy mixture containing marble chips. The soil should preferably be covered with pebbles. The growing season is in summer; each year only one pair of leaves is developed. The large flowers of the various species appear in the autumn, usually in the colours red, pink or yellow.

In winter they should be kept dry at a temperature of 10 °C. In summer, too, it is essential to water sparingly.

Arthrocereus campos-portoi   *Astrophytum myriostigma*

ARTHROCEREUS CAMPOS-PORTOI

Four species of the Arthrocereus ('jointed cereus') genus are known, mainly occurring in Brazil. They are graceful, often fairly dark-coloured cacti, usually low and columnar in habit. In mature plants the upper part of the root becomes woody. The flowers open only at night and are self-sterile. They are white in colour, long and slender, thinly covered in hairs; they are followed by juicy berries.

The species illustrated has brown spines; others, such as Arthrocereus mello-barretoi, are covered in greenish-yellow thorns.

Arthrocereus microsphaericus has a conspicuously large number of short, fine spines. As the name indicates, it is a low-growing species; microsphaericus alludes to the very small, almost spherical segments of which the stems are composed.

ASTROPHYTUM MYRIOSTIGMA (Bishop's Cap)

The Astrophytum genus includes only a few species, some of which are difficult to grow, suitable only for an expert collector. However, the Astrophytum myriostigma illustrated is reasonably easy to maintain.

The Bishop's Cap occurs in the northern part of Mexico, where it grows in the mountains even at fairly high altitudes (up to 2,500 m/8,000 ft). This cactus lacks thorns, but the ribs (usually five) are covered in a large number of fine white flakes. It is slow-growing, but may produce its pale yellow flowers (appearing in summer) when it has grown to only 8 cm (3 in.).

In summer it should be placed in a sunny window and watered moderately. In winter it prefers a temperature of 10–12°C and a dry atmosphere.

Astrophytum ornatum
Austrocylindropuntia verschaffeltii

ASTROPHYTUM ORNATUM

The botanical name Astrophytum means 'Star Plant' and the popular name 'Star Cactus' is therefore appropriate.

A. ornatum illustrated is the only commonly cultivated species of the genus whch has sharp thorns.

Astrophytum asterias, the Sea Urchin cactus, has a remarkable shape; it looks rather like a cake with the portions marked. It closely resembles Euphorbia obesa, illustrated on p. 71. In the nineteen-twenties very high prices were paid for these plants, but they are now less expensive.

This species is difficult to grow and is unsuitable for beginners. In summer it must be kept very warm. To bring it through the winter it is best kept dry at 10°C.

AUSTROCYLINDROPUNTIA VERSCHAFFELTII

For the sake of convenience this practically unpronounceable genus is sometimes classified among Opuntias, but the species differ from true Opuntias in that the joints are not flattened, but are usually cylinder- or club-shaped.

A. verschaffeltii originates in Bolivia and Argentina. The large, bright red flowers are 5 cm (2 in.) across.

Another species, A. vestita, has joints up to 25 cm (10 in.) in length, covered in long white hairs. This native of Bolivia has red flowers. There is also a freak strain called 'Cristata'.

For care, *see* Opuntia species.

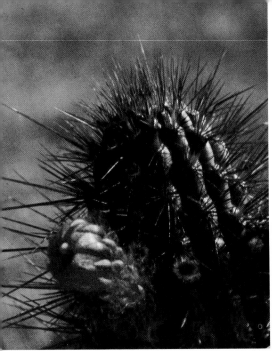

Borzicactus sepium

Brasiliopuntia brasiliensis

BORZICACTUS SEPIUM

This genus embraces a number of fairly low-growing, branched-columnar cacti. The flowers, usually red, open during the day. A particular feature is that the stamens are wooly-haired at the base.

Borzicactus sepium is fairly easy to grow and requires light shade. Normal potting compost, available in small packs, is satisfactory.

B. sepium grows wild in Peru and Ecuador. The specific name sepium means 'used for hedges', as it is planted for this purpose in Ecuador.

Another well-known species is B. icosagonus, from Peru. The stems, up to 50 cm (20 in.) in length and 6 cm ($2\frac{1}{2}$ in.) in diameter, are yellow-spined. The red flowers may grow to 8 cm (3 in.) across.

BRASILIOPUNTIA BRASILIENSIS (Brazilian opuntia)

The large Opuntia genus may be divided into four groups, namely those with flattened joints or 'pads', opuntia species with cylindrical stems, spherical opuntias, which are low-growing, and Brasiliopuntia, with branching cylindrical stems and thin leaf-like pads.

Brasiliopuntia brasiliensis, a native of tropical regions of South America, is the only species. The stem is round, the joints are flattened, often slightly wavy. The flowers are yellow. In its native habitat it grows into a tree, but in the living room it retains more modest proportions.

B. brasiliensis must not be placed in bright sunlight. The most favourable temperature in winter is between 10 and 20 °C.

Bryophyllum tubiflorum (detail of leaf-tip)   *Carnegiea gigantea*

BRYOPHYLLUM TUBIFLORUM

Bryophyllum species properly belong to the Kalanchoe genus, but the differences are so marked that they are better dealt with separately.

In Madagascar these plants grow wild. They are popular as house plants chiefly because of the fact that young plantlets develop at the tip of the cylindrical leaves (as in Bryophyllum tubiflorum) or along the leaf-edges (as in Bryophyllum daigremontianum). The flowers, orange-red in the former, lilac-coloured in the latter, are particularly fine.

Water normally in summer, sparingly in winter. Propagation from rooted plantlets. Be sure to grow a continuous supply of fresh plants, since mature specimens become unsightly.

CARNEGIEA GIGANTEA

This species, a giant among columnar cacti, occurs in Arizona, where it may grow to 10 or 15 m (30–50 feet) in height. It does not readily branch, although a few erect-growing side shoots grow from the upper half, giving the plant the shape of a candelabrum.

Carnegiea is a slow-growing cactus; gigantea is its only species. Such a genus, of which only one species is known, is called monotypic.

Carnegiea requires a fairly warm environment. In winter, too, the temperature should not drop much below 12 °C. Water sparingly and place in the best possible light.

Cephalocereus palmeri

Cephalocereus senilis

CEPHALOCEREUS PALMERI

If you wish the Cephalocereus species in your collection to flower, you should choose either C. palmeri or C. chrysacanthus. The former has white flowers merging into pink, the flowers of the latter are reddish in colour. Neither species flowers readily, but it does happen on occasion. In Cephalocereus palmeri the body is blue-bloomed, the spines are yellow. The species is covered in white hairs. Bear in mind that hairy cacti will thrive only in porous soil and it is therefore advisable to mix some gravel with the potting medium.

These species are sometimes classified in the genus Pilosocereus.

CEPHALOCEREUS SENILIS (Old Man Cactus)

I'm afraid you are never likely to have the pleasure of seeing your Old Man Cactus in bloom, for Cephalocereus senilis will not flower until it is at least 5 m (16 feet) tall. Because of its soft, white, hair-like spines it is very popular and it is therefore found in nearly every collection. The Old Man requires plenty of light and a slightly humid atmosphere. In winter it must be kept dry; the temperature should not drop below 7 °C. It is advisable to repot young plants every year, keeping the soil-ball intact as far as possible. This cactus may be grown from seed.

Cereus jamacaru

Cereus peruvianus

CEREUS JAMACARU

This very tall Cereus species occurs wild in Brazil. Actually it is a tree with a widespread crown, consisting of four- to six-ribbed branches. Initially the branches are blue-bloomed, forming a fine background to the numerous brown thorns. In the wild (but not in your living-room) this cactus produces white flowers up to 30 cm (12 in.) across. The 'Monstruosus' strain, which is crest-forming, is well worth growing.

Other valuable species are C. chalybaeus, C. validus and C. forbesii.

All the species mentioned above are undemanding as regards care. They may be grown in full sun and appreciate an occasional 'shower'. In summer they may be placed out of doors; in winter a temperature of about 8 °C is adequate, provided the plants are placed in good light.

CEREUS PERUVIANUS

At one time only columnar cacti were classified in the genus Cereus, but Cereus has now been sub-divided into several genera and itself includes only a few species, of which C. peruvianus is the best known.

This species is really far too large for the living-room, for it may grow to as much as 15 m (50 feet). The flowers, which usually open at night, appear only in mature plants. A striking, bluish waxy layer covers the entire body.

The freak forms are particularly suitable for use as house plants. 'Rock cactus' is an appropriate name for Cereus peruvianus 'Monstruosus'. The spines of this irregularly shaped cactus are short and inconspicuous.

Ceropegia woodii   *Ceropegia radicans (flowers among Euphorbia)*

CEROPEGIA WOODII (Hearts Entangled)

Few plants, and certainly few succulents, have more remarkable flowers than Ceropegia species. They are lantern-shaped, but there are considerable differences between the various species. The best known, Ceropegia woodii, is a native of south-eastern Africa. It has thread-like stems hanging down like a curtain and bearing small cormlets, in addition to beautifully shaped small leaves and flowers. If a stem with such a cormlet is detached and potted, it will grow into a new plant. The corm may grow to a diameter of 5 cm (2 in.). They grow best in a south-facing window. Water sparingly, even in summer.

CEROPEGIA RADICANS

Although the plant described above is the best known, there are about 160 other Ceropegia species which, unfortunately, are rarely encountered. They occur in dry regions of Africa, Asia, Northern Australia and elsewhere. Many of them are of creeping habit, but some have winding stems.

Ceropegia radicans has green flowers striped with white and reddish-purple.

In some species the tubular corolla widens at the base. Often the entrance to the widened section is barred by stiff hairs, so that insects (such as carrion flies, attracted by the disagreeable scent) can enter freely, but cannot easily get out. In their efforts to escape they encourage pollination. The hairs dry up at a later stage, but by then they have performed their function.

56

Chamaecereus silvestrii

Cleistocactus albisetus

CHAMAECEREUS SILVESTRII

This cactus, sometimes called the Peanut Cactus, originates in north-western Argentina. It is a clump-forming plant, built up from pale green branches.

The flowering season occurs in spring, when the vermilion-red flowers appear in great profusion. During the growing season light, warmth and water are indispensable, but in winter the temperature may drop almost to zero, provided the environment is well-lit and dry.

The plant is easily propagated by detaching and potting separate shoots.

Cristate forms and forms lacking chlorophyll must be grafted.

CLEISTOCACTUS ALBISETUS

The Greek word 'kleistos' means closed and this explains the generic name Cleistocactus, for the petals do not open.

Unusually in cacti, Cleistocactus species prefer a humid environment. This applies not only in summer: in winter, too, they must never be kept entirely dry, for they would quickly shrivel up. In addition they require a sunny position and nutritious soil.

Apart from C. albisetus, C. baumannii and the readily-flowering C. dependens are also worth growing. Probably best known is C. strausii, which has crimson flowers.

Conophytum compressum

Copiapoa humilis

CONOPHYTUM COMPRESSUM

For most Conophytum species the growing season does not start until late in summer. It is therefore essential to give them adequate moisture and, of course, light. In the dormant season in spring and summer they must be screened from bright sunlight.

The plant consists of spherical or cone-shaped bodies, sometimes flattened. In some species the two leaves are joined together and only a narrow split betrays the fact that the plant consists of two parts.

At a certain stage the bodies will dry up and shrivel, and a new pair of leaves will grow between. The large flowers are yellow, white or red and appear as the young plants develop.

COPIAPOA HUMILIS

Species of the Copiapoa genus occur only in northern Chile. They are particularly fine cacti, which will develop best if seedlings are grafted on stock. This procedure encourages flowering. The flattish flowers are yellow and appear in summer.

Copiapoa cinerea, covered in white meal, is a particularly striking species.

Other fine species are C. haseltoniana (grey-green), C. echinoides (initially the thorns are dark, later they turn grey) and C. humilis illustrated here, which is small and compact.

They should be carefully watered—only in warm and sunny weather. Do not pour water over the top.

Coryphantha bumamma   *Coryphantha clava*

CORYPHANTHA BUMAMMA

At first sight Coryphantha species resemble the well-known Mammillarias, and some people regard them as intermediate between Echinocactus and Mammillaria.

There are many species, all natives of the south-western part of the United States and of Mexico. They are remarkable for their numerous tubercles and often very beautiful spines.

C. bumamma is closely related to C. elephantidens, which has very large pink flowers. The flowers of C. bumamma are smaller and yellow in colour.

Coryphanthas are subject to attacks by red spider. The risk of infection may be reduced by spraying the plants in the growing season.

CORYPHANTHA CLAVA

Coryphantha species are conveniently divided into two groups, widely differing as regards the situation required and consequently also as regards care. The species of one group come from dry deserts. They are recognized by their stronger spine formation and are difficult to cultivate. A soil mixture containing a large proportion of gravel and practically lacking in organic substances is essential. In addition they tolerate very little water.

Other Coryphantha species require more moisture, at least in the growing season, and need a soil mixture fairly rich in humus, for they grow wild in grassy regions.

However, all species must be kept dry in a well-lit, cool position in winter.

Coryphantha clava has nectar glands in the axils of the tubercles and is therefore attractive to ants.

Cotyledon decussata (flower detail)   *Crassula arborescens*

COTYLEDON DECUSSATA

Cotyledon is a remarkable genus of leaf- and stem-succulents. The latter are rarely cultivated. Of these, Cotyledon fascicularis (syn. Cotyledon paniculata) is the largest; this South African 'butter tree' may grow to 1.5 m ($4\frac{1}{2}$ feet). The trunks are so soft (as soft as butter!) that they are easily cut.

Cotyledon orbiculata, a leaf succulent, has variable, thickly bloomed leaves, fading into red at the margin. The flowers grow in clusters and are yellow and red in colour.

C. decussata illustrated here originates in South-West Africa and may flower magnificently.

Cotyledons are grown in heavy, preferably clayey, soil. In summer they need plenty of sun; in winter they must be kept fairly dry, cool and in good light.

CRASSULA ARBORESCENS

Most Crassula species, including C. arborescens, are foliage plants. The growing season is in spring and summer. In late May or early June the plant may safely be put out of doors if you can give it a sunny and sheltered position. If you plant it out in the soil, watering may be restricted to a minimum. In late September the plant should be brought indoors and kept through the winter at a low temperature.

In nearly all books on house plants, the species described and illustrated as Crassula arborescens is a different one, actually C. portulacea. This green Crassula, also tree-like in shape, produces small white flowers, but only when mature.

Crassula lycopodioides   *Cylindropuntia leptocaulis*

CRASSULA LYCOPODIOIDES

Because of its unusual appearance this popular plant is often combined with other succulents and cacti in bowl collections.

It is fairly tolerant of sunshine, but must be protected against very bright rays. In summer it is watered 3 or 4 times a week; in winter once a fortnight is more than sufficient.

It is best repotted in early spring, just before the start of the growing season. The plant is easily increased, either by division or from cuttings. There are several strains of this species, which originates in South Africa.

CYLINDROPUNTIA LEPTOCAULIS

In this species with its long, thin, green joints, the thorns are surrounded by papery sheaths. The flowers are yellow-green in colour.

Cylindropuntia bigelowii is thickly spined and grows to 1 m ($3\frac{1}{4}$ feet) in height. The main branch and several side branches are easily distinguished. The violet-red flowers also develop at the top of the plant.

A striking species is C. tunicata, which is densely covered in thorns in papery sheaths. The spines are minutely barbed, and easily catch in the skin. They are painful to remove and the plant is therefore not very popular among growers and florists. It grows to 50–60 cm (20–25 in.) and has yellow flowers.

Cylindropuntia species require a warm and sunny position, but must be kept cool in winter.

Delosperma echinatum   *Dolichothele sphaerica*

DELOSPERMA ECHINATUM

This genus includes a large number of dwarf shrubs, of which only a few are suitable for use as house plants. One of these is D. echinatum (= like a hedgehog, spiny) (illustrated). This South African species makes a particularly attractive hanging plant and it is a pity that it is so rarely available at the florist's. It is one of those plants of which you must beg a cutting from a friendly fellow-collector.

The growing season is in summer; the plant may then be grown out of doors. The fairly small, white to yellow flowers appear practically throughout the year.

Delosperma lehmannii, a rare species, has larger flowers; the leaves are bare, whereas in D. echinatum they are irregularly covered in hairs.

DOLICHOTHELE SPHAERICA

A remarkable species belonging to the Mammillaria group; it originates in Texas. The plants are distinguished by their long, cylindrical tubercles and large flowers; these have a funnel-shaped tube. The plants are soft to the touch and therefore particularly susceptible to red spider. They have a thick taproot.

The best known species is Dolichothele longimamma, with yellow flowers. Other popular species sometimes placed in this genus, but having much smaller whitish flowers are D. camptotricha, which has strongly twisted thorns, and D. decipiens in which the thorns are straight.

These cacti may be grown in a normal cactus mixture. They should be watered like Mammillaria. Avoid bright sunlight; a slightly shady situation is best.

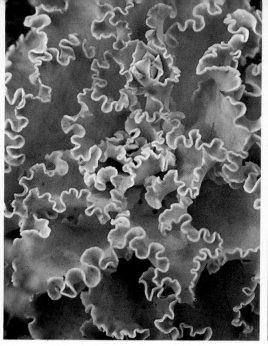

Echeveria gibbiflora 'Crispata'　　　　　　　　　　*Echeveria pumila 'Glauca'*

ECHEVERIA GIBBIFLORA 'CRISPATA'

This is a large and vigorous species. The leaves may grow to 20 cm (8 in.) in length and 15 cm (6 in.) across and are covered in fine thorns. The branched inflorescence appears on a tall stalk and the bright red flowers are a veritable ornament in the living-room.

Echeveria agavoides is an unusual species, a native of Mexico. This plant develops rosettes up to 20 cm (8 in.) across. The green leaves are triangular in shape. The inflorescence consists of long plumes of numerous red and yellow flowers.

Another fine species is E. elegans, which has played its part in the creation of innumerable hybrids. The plant itself has bluish-white leaves, covered with white meal, and pink and yellow flowers.

Echeveria fulgens produces bright red flowers and grey-green leaves without bloom.

ECHEVERIA PUMILA 'GLAUCA'

Many plant lovers know this species also by the name Echeveria glauca. Like Echeveria setosa it was for a long time used as a bedding plant. The bloomed leaves are bluish-white in colour. The flowers are rose-red, tipped with yellow.

E. harmsii is a species with large red and yellow flowers often marketed under the name Oliveranthus elegans. The species mentioned are all natives of Mexico.

Do not give Echeveria species too much water, for this may cause rotting at the base and, in some species, mildew. The plants should be placed in full sunlight.

Echeveria setosa   *Echinocactus grusonii*

ECHEVERIA SETOSA

The history of this plant in cultivation does not go back very far. It was not introduced in Europe until the present century and was initially used as a bedding plant.

This succulent does not require much warmth; it is happy in a cool room. In summer a sunny spot is advisable.

This native of Mexico has a magnificent inflorescence; the flowers which appear in spring and early summer, are red, with yellow tips.

Crossing E. setosa with E. derenbergii has resulted in a hybrid called Echeveria 'Derosa', in which the leaves are grey-green and almost bare, while the flowers are orange.

ECHINOCACTUS GRUSONII (Golden Barrel cactus)

Some collections contain specimens nearly a metre in diameter. The species originates in Mexico and has striking, golden-yellow thorns which show up to advantage against the green body of the cactus.

These plants are easily raised from seed and will grow rapidly in nutritious soil. The seeds should be sown in special cactus compost, which can be bought in small quantities. It is advisable to cover the seed-pans with glass. Ensure a measure of bottom heat by placing them on a window-sill above a central heating radiator. The temperature should be between 20° and 30°C.

In summer, unless placed out-of-doors the plant must be protected against very bright sunlight, otherwise it may get scorched. In winter it should be kept at a temperature of 8 to 10°C and only watered very occasionally and sparingly.

Echinocereus pulchellus   *Echinocereus triglochidiatus*

ECHINOCEREUS PULCHELLUS

At one time this genus, which embraces about 60 species, was considered part of the Cereus genus. These plants are very popular among collectors, especially because of the modest size of most of the species, and because of the fairly large, splendidly coloured flowers.

Echinocereus pulchellus is initially spherical in shape, but later becomes shortly cylindrical. If grafted it may flower at a very early age. The flowers of this species are pink in colour and 3 to 4 cm (1–1½ in.) across.

This fine cactus requires a warm and sunny environment and (for a cactus) a fair amount of water, at any rate in the growing period. In winter cool and dry conditions, in the best possible light, are an absolute 'must'.

ECHINOCEREUS TRIGLOCHIDIATUS (Claret-Cup or Strawberry Cactus)

The genus Echinocereus includes green, lightly spined species, densely thorned species and even hairy forms. The care they require varies considerably. The two latter groups need a dry and sunny situation. The bare forms tolerate a little more water and do better in a slightly shady spot; this means that they are easier to grow.

E. triglochidiatus is found in Arizona and Texas and has globular to cylindrical stems. The flowers are up to 7 cm (2¾ in.) in length and fairly broad.

E. fendleri, from Mexico, has pale to deep purple flowers.

The flowers of E. dasyacanthus are yellow; this plant is regarded as one of the finest species of the genus.

Echinofossulocactus coptonogonus   *Echinomastus macdowellii*

ECHINOFOSSULOCACTUS COPTONOGONUS

Although this polysyllabic genus presents the classifier with a number of problems, the plants are not difficult to grow. Provide nutritious soil, adequate moisture (by cactus standards) and protection against very bright sunlight in summer. Add a resting period in a well-lit situation in winter, and you will have satisfied all their requirements.

The cactus body grows to a maximum diameter of 10 cm (4 in.) and usually consists of numerous ribs, although the species illustrated only has 10 to 14. The flowers, about 3 cm (1 in.) in length, are white with crimson striped petals.

Another species, more or less spherical in shape, is E. crispatus, which has more ribs and produces violet-coloured flowers.

ECHINOMASTUS MACDOWELLII

Of this genus few species are known. They are fairly small, spherical or squat and cylindrical in shape, and densely covered in thorns.

One well-known species is Echinomastus macdowellii. It may grow to 6 or 7 cm ($2\frac{1}{4}$ to $2\frac{3}{4}$ in.) in height and in the course of time will attain a diameter of 10 cm (4 in.). The little plant is covered in a veritable carpet of criss-cross spines. The funnel-shaped flower is pinkish in colour.

These cacti are satisfied with little moisture and in summer may be placed in full sunlight.

The area of distribution of Echinomastus species is confined to northern Mexico and the adjacent United States.

Echinopsis aurea   *Echinopsis 'Yascot'*

ECHINOPSIS AUREA

This genus occurs in Paraguay, Uruguay, Bolivia and Argentina, but on your window-sill, too, they will give of their best. They are vigorous growers and in addition may put forth fine, trumpet-shaped flowers in the colours white, lilac, pink and yellow. An extra bonus is their pleasant scent.

Echinopsis species are easily increased. They produce side-shoots which may be detached and inserted in sandy soil after the cut has been left to dry for a few days.

These cacti enjoy a soil mixture fairly rich in humus. In summer they appreciate some feeding; in winter they must be kept practically dry. E. aurea occurs in western Argentina.

ECHINOPSIS 'YASCOT'

Initially most Echinopsis species are spherical in shape, but eventually they become shortly columnar. Man's influence—and more particularly the activities of cactus growers—has had important consequences for the genus. Wild-growing species are commonly found in cultivation, but innumerable hybrids have also been produced. The one illustrated is believed to be the result of crossing Pseudolobivia and Echinopsis.

As a rule the flower-buds develop after the dormant season; their appearance is the signal for a slight increase in the water supply. Most forms are night-flowering, or at least wait until evening before they open their flowers. They close in the morning and rarely re-open more than once.

Epiphyllum hybrid   *Epiphyllum hybrid*

EPIPHYLLUM HYBRIDS (Leaf cactus, Phyllocactus)

Epiphyllum used to be called Phyllocactus and is sometimes still wrongly known by that name. As regards their natural habitat the species differ considerably from their relatives. They are quite exceptional in that, like bromeliads and many orchids, they are epiphytes, that is to say that they grow on trees but take no nourishment from them. They are found in the forests of Central and South America.

Several Epiphyllum species are cultivated, but many Hybrids have been produced by crossing them with Heliocereus, Selenicereus, Nopalxochia and others; these produce flowers in many colours (red, pink, orange, white). The flowers appear only on well developed joints. To encourage flowering, a resting period at about 8 °C is essential from November to the end of February. At this time little water should be given and the plant must not be fed. Occasional careful syringing with tepid water is, however, desirable. When the flower-buds are beginning to form, the plant should not be turned in relation to the direction of the light.

The magnificent flowers now appear; when they are finished, the plant must be encouraged to grow. Adequate watering and regular feeding are essential at this time. From early June until September the plant is put in a sheltered, slightly shady spot in the garden. Repotting should preferably be undertaken after the flowering season; standard potting compost is suitable.

Eriocereus bonplandii

Espostoa lanata

ERIOCEREUS BONPLANDII

In the Argentine, where they grow wild, Eriocereus species develop into veritable thickets. They are fairly rampant growers, usually producing limp, sometimes climbing, branches. Large specimens are occasionally seen covering the walls of greenhouses. The flowers resemble those of the Queen of the Night cactus and, like these, do not display their beauty until nightfall.

E. bonplandii may flower when it is only 50 cm (20 in.) tall.

Another well-known species, E. jusbertii (probably a hybrid) is very popular among cactus growers because it provides excellent stock on which to graft all sorts of less vigorous species.

Eriocereus species require nutritious soil, adequate moisture, and sunshine. In winter the temperature should be kept at 8–10 °C.

ESPOSTOA LANATA

This remarkable woolly cactus originates in Peru, as do its fellow species. It is loved especially for its silky white hairs which cover the plant like a wig; this even applies to small young plants.

In Peru it may grow into a tree several metres (10 to 15 feet) in height and may then produce very pale pink flowers from the sides of the trunk.

The plant flowers at night, but in this country we cannot hope to see this happening. However, I have read that it may occur in Mediterranean countries where the plant is in cultivation.

Its requirements are: sun, adequate water and nutritious soil.

69

Euphorbia bupleurifolia   *Euphorbia grandicornis*

EUPHORBIA BUPLEURIFOLIA

This strange looking plant, consisting merely of a short, hard trunk, topped by a tuft of thin, narrow leaves, once again confirms the variability in form of the genus. The species requires porous soil, rich in humus, and slightly warmer and damper conditions than the other species. It should be kept dry in the dormant season, which starts when the leaves drop.

Euphorbia caput-medusae, a native of Cape Town's Table Mountain, is another strange looking species. The fat, globular main trunk produces numerous spiralling branches—hence the name Medusa head.

Cuttings from side branches will not grow into complete plants.

EUPHORBIA GRANDICORNIS

The Euphorbia genus is one of the largest in the plant world; it embraces approximately 2,000 species, including annuals, biennials and perennials, some of which flower profusely. Some are weeds, others valuable garden plants.

When not in flower, many of the succulent species are practically indistinguishable from cacti. Their identity is betrayed only by the milky substance they contain and by the absence of areoles. Large, bizarrely shaped specimens are much in demand; they appear to good advantage in a modern interior.

The Euphorbia grandicornis illustrated may grow into a beautiful shrub-sized plant. E. pseudocactus is a fine species for glass containers; it branches attractively and is easy to care for. Another stylish species is E. canariensis, which has dull green 4- or 5-sided branches.

70

Euphorbia milii   *Euphorbia obesa*

EUPHORBIA MILII (Crown of Thorns)

Together with the Poinsettia (Euphorbia pulcherrima), the Crown of Thorns is undoubtedly the most important indoor spurge. Dwarf forms are also available. Red bracts, growing in pairs, decorate the plant for much of the year; the actual flowers are barely visible. They appear in profusion especially between February and July.

Unlike most other succulent spurges, the Crown of Thorns may be kept in a heated living-room in winter. Occasionally the leaves suddenly turn yellow and drop; this means that the plant needs a rest and for about two months should be given very little water and no fertilizer. New leaves will soon develop.

New plants are easily grown from cuttings.

EUPHORBIA OBESA

This attractive species originates in South Africa and is hardly distinguishable from Astrophytum asterias. Another unusual species is Euphorbia globosa. Both belong to the group which includes several dwarf, globular or short cylindrical species. The 'globes' are only a few centimetres across, but larger joints may develop. In the course of time the plant may form a complete collection of these little balls, at first dark green, later turning very pale. Initially a few small leaves appear, but these soon-drop. Both species require a well-lit, sunny situation. They should be kept dry in not too cold a spot in winter.

Faucaria tigrina

Ferocactus glaucescens

FAUCARIA TIGRINA (Tiger's Chaps)

This is an attractive house plant, provided you look after it properly. It needs a fair amount of water and plenty of warmth and light during its short growing season in summer. When the large yellow flowers appear in the autumn—as a rule they do not open until the afternoon—the growing season proper is at an end. The plant should then be kept dry in a fresh and cool environment; good light is essential in this period. Make sure the soil is porous, for excess water causes rotting.

The F. tigrina illustrated is only one of about thirty species, occurring in the arid eastern part of the Cape Province.

Other species to be recommended are F. tuberculosa, which has very knobbly leaves, and the pale blue-green F. britteniae.

FEROCACTUS GLAUCESCENS

Ferocactus is a truly savage genus. Ferox means fierce, and in fact these cacti produce strong, heavy thorns, broad and horny in some species. Usually they are globular to cylindrical in shape. The area of distribution of the genus is the S.W. United States and Mexico.

These plants grow very slowly. The species illustrated has straight, pure yellow spines. Another fine, horny species is Ferocactus latispinus, which puts forth magnificent rose-red, bell-shaped flowers; unfortunately this happens only rarely, but the striking red, hooked central spines largely make up for it.

Ferocactus stainesii

Gasteria verrucosa

FEROCACTUS STAINESII

According to some books on the subject, this Mexican cactus may grow to as much as 3 m (10 ft) in height. The central spines are bodkin-shaped, while the surrounding spines take the form of long hairs. The flowers are orange-red.

Another fine species is Ferocactus emoryi; this has scarlet central spines and knobbly ribs. You might be interested to learn that the Amerindians used the barbed spines of some Ferocactus species as fish hooks.

Ferocactus species grow best in clayey soil. They should be placed in a sunny and warm position; in summer regular watering is essential, but in winter they must be kept fairly dry.

GASTERIA VERRUCOSA

In most Gasteria species the leaves grow in two planes, which makes them suitable for a narrow window-sill, even though they may grow quite large in the course of time.

The fine inflorescence consists of slender racemes. In summer the plants may be placed in a sunny, sheltered position in the garden. They like to spend the winter in a temperature of 8–10°C; during that time they should be watered sparingly. Some species, for instance Gasteria verrucosa, were already grown in botanical gardens 250 years ago.

The leaves are covered in innumerable white warts. The plant is easily propagated from offshoots which appear in large numbers and strike fairly readily. Gasteria maculata is another well-known species; G. liliputana is a very small dwarf form.

Glottiphyllum semicylindricum

Graptopetalum paraguayense

GLOTTIPHYLLUM SEMICYLINDRICUM

This genus embraces about 60 species, occurring in South and South-West Africa, where they grow in the most arid places. They should be treated accordingly: although difficult customers, they can nevertheless be grown (and brought into flower) indoors. To this end they must be kept fairly dry, even in summer, but given plenty of light and (frequently also) sun. They should be screened only from the fiercest rays. The soil may be poor and should be mixed with at least an equal quantity of sand. The flowers, usually yellow, appear between August and January.

One of the smallest species is called Glottiphyllum oligocarpum.

GRAPTOPETALUM PARAGUAYENSE

This succulent, originating in Arizona, is closely related to Sedum and Echeveria and is equally simple to grow. Normal soil mixture and a fair amount of water in summer provide the correct growing conditions. In winter the plants may be put in a cool position, provided the soil is kept dry. However, they may also remain in the living-room.

In its native habitat it is a small, freely branching shrub. Greyish-white leaves, arranged in rosettes, grow from the trunks; they turn violet in the sun.

The inflorescence consists of widely spaced, creamy white flowers tipped with purple.

This species has been crossed with various Echeveria species including E. amoena; the resultant hybrid is called × Graptoveria 'Acaulis'.

74

Gymnocalycium mihanovichii 'Orange'   *Gymnocalycium pflanzii*

GYMNOCALYCIUM MIHANOVICHII

The craze for brightly coloured, grafted cacti has reached us from Japan. They are grown in tens of thousands, usually grafted on Hylocereus. They are incapable of an independent existence, since they lack powers of assimilation.

The full name of this plant is Gymnocalycium mihanovichii var. friedrichii, and numerous forms exist under the names 'Hibotan', 'Red Cap', 'Black Cap', 'Yellow Cap', etc. Their lifespan is restricted; they should really be re-grafted after about two years. Occasionally they put forth a few pale flowers.

Keep them out of bright sunlight and in summer water fairly freely. In winter they must be kept dry.

GYMNOCALYCIUM PFLANZII

The Gymnocalycium genus originates in South America. They are rewarding plants to grow, especially since most species are capable of flowering at an early age. The photograph shows Gymnocalycium pflanzii, a greatly valued species.

The species G. andreae grows to a maximum diameter of 5 cm (2 in.); the greenish-yellow flower appearing at the top is of equal size.

As the name implies, G. multiflorum flowers profusely; the flowers are pale pink in colour.

The dull grey species G. baldianum has red flowers. As you see, there is plenty of choice.

75

Haageocereus pseudomelanostele   *Hatiora salicornioides*

HAAGEOCEREUS PSEUDOMELANOSTELE

Of all columnar cacti the species belonging to this genus are probably the easiest to grow. They have few pretensions: somewhat clayey soil, a very sunny situation, not too cool in winter—these are their minimal requirements. They are grown on their own roots as well as grafted on stock (e.g. Eriocereus jusbertii). The latter is advisable to achieve regular growth.

There are quite a few species, though these are divided into groups: those originating in coastal deserts, which have a creeping habit, and the more erect growing forms which occur among rocks. Their natural habitat is in Peru. The white, red and greenish flowers have long tubes. As a rule the flowers open at night.

HATIORA SALICORNIOIDES

This is not an easy plant to grow, since it is an epiphyte in nature. To see it growing in this way, you'd have to go to Brazil, where some firms develop pendulous twigs up to 1 m ($3\frac{1}{4}$ feet) in length.

In cultivation it remains much smaller and the usual form has more erect branches. The orange-yellow flowers, which later fade to pink, are well worth seeing, though only 1 cm (less than $\frac{1}{2}$ in.) across.

In view of its epiphytic character I'd advise you to add a large quantity of humus to its soil. This cactus should be watered a little more generously than is usual for cacti. It should preferably be given a slightly shady position.

Haworthia margaritifera　　　　　　　　　　　*Haworthia reinwardtii*

HAWORTHIA MARGARITIFERA

Among lovers of succulents Haworthia species are extremely popular. Like Gasteria, Aloe, etc. they belong to the Lily family. The plant itself gives no indication of this fact, but it becomes more obvious when the flowers appear. All the (very numerous) species originate in South Africa.

The plant illustrated (above left) forms firm little rosettes, consisting of many thick, sharply pointed leaves. It owes its popularity to the pearly tubercles on the leaves.

Mature plants produce small offset rosettes, which are easily detached and grown separately. In winter they should be given only the minimum amount of water.

HAWORTHIA REINWARDTII

Haworthia species may be grown in positions where they never receive any sun, though light is, of course, essential. Some vigorous species may be put in the garden in summer, provided they are kept out of bright sunlight.

These succulents do best in very clayey soil. In hot weather they may be watered fairly generously. As they have a shallow root system half-pots or pans are most suitable.

The form illustrated belongs to the group of cylindrical species; they grow to 15–20 cm (6–8 in.).

Haworthia tortuosa is another attractive plant. The fairly elongate leaves grow in three spiralling rows.

Hoya bella   *Hoya carnosa*

HOYA BELLA (Small Wax Flower)

You may wonder whether the wax flower plants properly belong in this book, since they are found in every book on house plants. On the other hand, they definitely have succulent foliage, so their inclusion is justified. The genus Hoya occurs from southern China to Australia.

Make sure that this attractive hanging plant is always left undisturbed (preferably in the morning sun), since otherwise the flowers are likely to drop, in which case we cannot enjoy their delicious scent.

Regular spray-misting, using tepid water, will keep the plant in prime condition. In addition it requires a fairly high temperature. An occasional dose of plant-food (except in the period when the flower-buds are forming) is desirable.

HOYA CARNOSA (Wax flower)

Only three of the many Hoya species, called after the English grower Thomas Hoy, are in common cultivation, and of these H. carnosa is the *primus inter pares*. As a rule it is trained on wire bent into a loop.

Experience has shown that this wax flower does best near an east-facing window. A south-facing window is also suitable, provided the plant is screened against bright sunlight. This species, too, should be moved as little as possible, and in other ways as well should be cared for like H. bella. The flowers, which in warm weather frequently contain many drops of nectar, appear in the period June–October. Variegated forms, such as 'Variegata' and 'Exotica' flower less profusely.

Huernia hystrix   *Kalanchoe beharensis*

HUERNIA HYSTRIX

Together with the much better known Stapelia and the uncommon Caralluma, Huernia belongs to the group of so-called carrion flowers. The flowers, usually five-petalled and varying considerably in size, colour and marking, have a very disagreeable smell of decaying meat; this smell attracts carrion flies which pollinate the plants.

As a rule the stems of Huernia species are square to hexagonal; they rarely grow beyond 8 cm (3 in.) in height. In some species the flowers are conspicuously marked with beautiful stripes. Others have yellow and red blotched, or whitish with purply-red flowers. They appear in summer at the base of the plants.

Huernia species are sensitive to excess water, but are otherwise not difficult to grow.

KALANCHOE BEHARENSIS

In spite of the fact that this plant soon loses its lower foliage, it may nevertheless be a real ornament in the living-room, for new, beautifully shaped leaves constantly develop at the top; the surface is almost felty. In the course of time the stem turns woody, clearly showing the scars of dropped leaves. Like most of the approximately twenty species, Kalanchoe beharensis is a native of Madagascar.

Kalanchoe species will thrive in most soil mixtures. In summer the plant may be placed in full sun out of doors, where it must be watered fairly generously. In winter watering should be restricted to a minimum, for serious loss of foliage may be the result of overwatering during that period. You have been warned.

Kalanchoe blossfeldiana 'Tom Thumb' *Kalanchoe tomentosa*

KALANCHOE BLOSSFELDIANA

Normally the flowering season of Kalanchoe begins in February—March, for it is a short-day plant; that is, the flowerbuds are formed in the period when there are few hours of daylight. By artificially shortening the day, growers are able to bring the plants into flower at other times as well. Sometimes it is necessary to give them artificial light in order to delay flowering.

It is fairly simple to maintain these plants in good condition in the living-room. Keep them fairly cool and in summer protect them against bright sunlight. The dormant season starts in October and continues until the new flowers appear. The soil-ball should be kept constantly, but moderately, moist. After flowering the plant may be cut back fairly drastically.

Strains with coarser leaves and orange, yellow and red flowers are also available.

KALANCHOE TOMENTOSA

This species rarely flowers in cultivation, but in any case the yellowish-brown flowers are fairly inconspicuous. On the other hand it has magnificent felty foliage. At the tips of the leaves the hairs are brown and my children used to say they were 'burnt'. The hairy down is at its best if the plant is placed in bright sunlight.

In its country of origin (Madagascar) this Kalanchoe may grow to nearly a metre (3 feet) in height; in that case the freely branching plant will turn woody at the base.

In winter it should be given a well-lit and not too warm situation (to 10°C). New plants are easily grown from leaf cuttings as well as by other methods.

Lampranthus roseus

Leuchtenbergia principis

LAMPRANTHUS ROSEUS (Midday Flower)

This plant is closely related to Cryophytum cristallinum (Ice plant), that well-known garden plant with its pearly leaves and soft pastel-coloured flowers. It is native to South Africa.

Lampranthus should be grown in full sun, both in summer and in winter. During June, July and August the pots may be placed out of doors. Often the pink flowers appear in great profusion.

L. blandus, also native to South Africa, is easily grown from cuttings at any time of the year, except during the winter months. Cuttings 6–8 cm ($2\frac{1}{2}$–3 in.) are inserted in a sandy mixture; about five cuttings in a fairly large pot will produce a fine effect.

LEUCHTENBERGIA PRINCIPIS

Leuchtenbergia is a monotypic genus, i.e. there is only one known species. This is L. principis, which occurs in central and northern Mexico.

In structure it is one of the most remarkable cacti known. It appears to have leaves and in this respect somewhat resembles certain Agave and Aloe species. The leaf-shaped lower tubercles gradually dry out and eventually drop, giving the plant a short trunk.

As a rule this cactus, which grows to about 50 cm (20 in.), does not branch, but occasionally it branches and with its yellow flowers may form a great asset in any collection. Grafted on vigorous stock it grows better than on its own roots.

In summer it requires plenty of sun and warmth; in winter it must be kept cool and dry.

Lithops fulleri

Lithops salicola

LITHOPS FULLERI (Living Stones)

The beautifully marked Lithops fulleri produces small white flowers at some time between July and December. The flowers will open only in adequate warmth and sunlight and then only in the afternoon. After flowering the two leaves gradually shrivel up; a new pair of leaves develops in between, initially protected by the shrivelled leaves which do not disappear completely until the summer. Once the young leaves are clearly visible, the plant may be carefully watered in sunny, warm weather. Make sure no water falls on or between the leaves.

To keep the soil as pure as possible and to avoid rotting, it is advisable to cover the soil-ball with fine gravel.

LITHOPS SALICOLA (Living stones)

The name Lithops is derived from two Greek words: *lithos*, a stone, and *ops*, the face, and was chosen because of the resemblance of the plants to the pebbles amongst which they often grow. The popular name of these very succulent little plants is therefore quite appropriate. The numerous species occur in South Africa and South West Africa in regions of low rainfall, especially in the Karroo.

Some Lithops species withdraw almost entirely underground during prolonged periods of drought. The plants absorb the necessary light via a small 'window' of transparent cell tissue.

In summer the plant requires plenty of sun; water sparingly. In winter it must be given a well-lit cool position and should be kept dry.

Lobivia cinnabarina

Lobivia pentlandii

LOBIVIA CINNABARINA

Lobivia species occur, among other places, in Bolivia. When this group of cacti was separated from the genus Echinopsis, the name Lobivia was invented: it is an anagram of Bolivia. Mediolobivia and Pseudolobivia are closely related.

Most Lobivia species are spherical in shape, but oblong forms also occur. About 70 species are known; their spine formation is not particularly beautiful, but they largely compensate by their extremely profuse flowering. The flowers appear in summer in the colours yellow, pink, red or white. Many of the species develop offsets, which are easily detached and grown into separate plants.

LOBIVIA PENTLANDII

When you first set out on the slippery path of cactus collection, you should try this (as well as other) Lobivia species. They will thrive even in a cold frame out of doors. In summer they need to be put under glass only when it rains a lot. You will be amazed at their resultant growth and flowering. In winter a cool, dry and well-lit position satisfies their requirements.

Lobivia pentlandii is the oldest known species. The flowers are orange-red, but occasionally occur in other colours. The flowers of L. jajoiana open for only a few hours, but are worth seeing: they are wine-red with a black heart. L. densispina has yellow, red or orange flowers, 6 cm ($2\frac{1}{2}$ in.) across.

Lophophora williamsii

Mamillopsis senilis

LOPOPHORA WILLIAMSII

This plant's kindly aspect (it has small tufts of white wool where one would expect spines) is deceptive, for it contains a very dangerous drug used by certain Indian tribes in Mexico in religious ceremonies. The drug leads to visions and great excitement; excessive doses may cause paralysis and unconsciousness. The Indian name for this cactus is Peyotl. Because of its properties it is sometimes regarded as a holy plant.

This cactus has a long taproot and, unless it is grafted, must be grown in a deep pot. In summer it needs fairly generous watering and a sunny situation. Of course it must be kept dry in winter.

MAMILLOPSIS SENILIS

It is a pity that this cactus so rarely flowers in the living-room, for the orange-red to violet petals with their dark central band are particularly beautiful.

However, the plant in itself is also attractive and ornamental. It is spherical in shape, covered almost entirely in soft, practically snow-white hairs. When it has reached a size of 6–8 cm (2½–3 in.) it develops side-shoots.

It occurs at high altitudes (to 3,000 m — 10,000 feet) in the mountains of N.W. Mexico, where in winter it can be covered in snow. It is difficult to cultivate. Be sure to keep it very cool and dry in winter.

Mammillaria pennispinosa　　　　　　　*Mammillaria dumetorum*

MAMMILLARIA PENNISPINOSA

This species, introduced in Europe fairly recently, forms tiny plants with thick taproots. Its feathery hairs make it attractive even when not in flower—a good reason to buy it. The flowers are whitish, with a pink centre. The best results are achieved if it is grown in full sun.

Mammillaria magnimamma is a particularly well-known species, found in large numbers in central Mexico. It is spherical in shape, with cone-shaped tubercles, which contain sap. The flowers are red, pink or white with a pink central stripe on the petals.

Mammillaria species are easily grown from seed. The fine seed grains should be covered by only the thinnest layer of the growing medium; cover the pot with glass.

MAMMILLARIA DUMETORUM

Most Mammillaria species are very easy to grow. They flower readily in the living-room and are attractive even when not in flower.

Their area of distribution is a large one: it includes Texas, New Mexico, Arizona, California, Colombia and the West Indies, but most species are found in Mexico.

Mammillaria dumetorum has short, yellowish spines and whitish flowers. The small red fruits, too, are most decorative.

A particularly interesting species is Mammillaria hahniana, sometimes called 'Old Lady' because of its long white hairs. The small rose-red flowers appear early in May.

Mammillaria spinosissima

Mammillaria zeilmanniana

MAMMILLARIA SPINOSISSIMA

In summer Mammillaria species need generous watering, but in winter they must be kept practically dry in a cool environment (6–8 °C) and the best possible light. During the growing season in summer they require regular and adequate doses of plant food. Most species require a very sunny position in summer; this improves the colour of the spines.

Mammillaria spinosissima is not merely beautiful: it is also very easy to grow.

It is closely related to M. rhodantha, from which it is not easily distinguished. Finally I should mention M. prolifera, which has creamy yellow flowers and is considered one of the simplest species to cultivate.

MAMMILLARIA ZEILMANNIANA

Mammillaria embraces about 250 species—more than any other genus of cacti. It is therefore understandable that there are collectors who specialize in these cacti. For the same reason you will understand that it has not been possible to illustrate more than four species in this book and that the number of species mentioned also had to be restricted. In addition to those mentioned and illustrated there are many others which thrive in cultivation. M. wildii is pale green and fairly 'tender'; it does not tolerate bright sunlight. The white to greenish flowers often appear in rings near the stem-apex. Mature plants consist of a large number of separate cylindrical stems.

M. zeilmanniana, which grows in globular-shaped clusters, produces small violet-red or white flowers.

Melocactus bahiensis

Melocactus rubrispinus

MELOCACTUS BAHIENSIS

I feel I should warn you that this cactus is very difficult to grow; even experienced collectors encounter problems.

The so-called 'coastal' forms (such as M. maxonii, M. violaceus and the M. bahiensis illustrated) require a well-lit, warm and, especially, humid environment. They should be kept close to the window throughout the year. In winter it is essential to keep them cool and fairly dry.

Great demands are also made on the soil, which must be light, porous and mixed with plenty of crushed brick or potsherds.

The area of distribution of these cacti stretches from Mexico to Brazil.

MELOCACTUS RUBRISPINUS

Melocactus species were among the earliest cacti known in Europe. Sailors visiting America after it was discovered were immediately attracted by these plants, so different from any they knew at home. Cacti moreover proved to be capable of withstanding long sea voyages and they therefore soon made their appearance in Europe, where they became greatly admired.

When these so-called 'melon' cacti come into flower, a cylindrical, bristly 'hat' develops at the top. This is called the cephalium; here the flowers will appear. You will rarely see this happening, for large imported plants do not often come into full flower and plants grown from seed frequently take 10 years before they flower.

Monvillea spegazzinii 'Cristata' *Myrtillocactus geometrizans*

MONVILLEA SPEGAZZINII

These cacti belong to the Cereus group. They are slender rib-stemmed cacti which deserve our attention even though most of them are not very suitable for living-room culture. M. spegazzinii and M. cavendishii are two of the species in cultivation. The former is a native of Paraguay and is easily recognized by its unusual blue-green colour, its white-blotched branches and its black thorns. Some books on the subject mention that this plant occasionally produces its elongated white and pink flowers when it is only a foot or so tall. M. cavendishii has large white flowers. It is sometimes used as grafting stock.

The specimen illustrated has been grafted on Hylocereus and is a so-called 'cristate' form. Water normally and protect against bright sunlight.

MYRTILLOCACTUS GEOMETRIZANS

This is a strongly branching columnar cactus originating in southern and central Mexico and in Guatemala. At one time it was included in the genus Cereus, along with Monvillea, Eriocereus, Echinocereus, Stetsonia, Trichocereus and others.

It may grow to 4m (13feet) and has fairly thick branches (up to 10cm—4in.—in diameter). However, in cultivation the branches are considerably thinner; the plant remains much smaller and does not flower. Its blue wax layer and its sparse spine formation are striking features.

This cactus should be watered normally; it requires slight shade and a minimum temperature of 8–10°C.

Neoporteria gerocephala *Nopalxochia phyllanthoides*

NEOPORTERIA GEROCEPHALA

Initially Neoporteria species are spherical in shape, but at a later stage they become slightly more cylindrical. They are popular mainly on account of their thorns (white, yellow, brown and black). They like a well-lit position and soil mixed with some clay. The species occur in Chile and in northern Argentina.

Because of its numerous, disorderly-growing long spines, the beautiful Neoporteria gerocephala is sometimes compared to the Old Man cactus. Its large flowers are carmine red.

Neoporteria subgibbosa, which has pink flowers, may also be recommended. Neoporteria species do best as house plants if they are grafted, preferably on stock of Eriocereus jusbertii.

NOPALXOCHIA PHYLLANTHOIDES

This brilliant cactus grows wild in Mexico. It is an epiphyte, which means that the soil mixture must contain at least 25 per cent of rotted leafmould. The leaves, which lack spine formation, are pale green, but in the sun turn reddish in colour. It should, however, not be grown in too sunny a spot, but in slight shade; in addition it requires a fair amount of water. Watering should be continued in winter, when the plant must not be kept cold. The magnificent rose-red flowers, at first fairly small, but larger at a later stage, may decorate the plant for a period of 8–10 weeks.

A large-flowering cultivar is marketed under the name 'German Empress'. The species is also crossed with Epiphyllum; the hybrid is very fine.

Notocactus haselbergii

Notocactus mammulosus

NOTOCACTUS HASELBERGII

It may be said without any reservation that the grafted specimen of Notocactus haselbergii (or, as it is sometimes known, Brasilicactus haselbergii) is one of the most popular species of the genus.

The same applies to Notocactus leninghausii (or Eriocactus leninghausii). This columnar species is densely covered in yellow spines. The flowers, too, are yellow. Cristate forms exist of Notocactus leninghausii and other species; these are grafted on Cereus stock to improve their vigour.

There are other interesting species, of which I shall mention only the tiny N. apricus and N. graessneri, which has greenish flowers.

These Notocactus species require nutritious soil, rich in humus.

NOTOCACTUS MAMMULOSUS

Notocactus species are very suitable for a beginner's collection. They are easily grown from seed and even young plants are capable of flowering. In summer they require a well-lit situation; they will even thrive out of doors in that season. They should be watered very sparingly even in the growing period. In winter they must be kept dry, but not too cold. A temperature of 12–14 °C is recommended.

The species illustrated is a particularly good one; its yellow flowers grow to 5 cm (2 in.) in length.

N. mammulosus var. submammulosus has slightly smaller flowers, but in most other respects resembles the typical variety.

Opuntia bergerana

Opuntia microdasys albispina

OPUNTIA BERGERANA

The origin of this species is unknown. It now occurs wild in northern Italy, but this cannot be its native habitat.

This pad cactus quickly grows too large for use in the living-room, but new joints may be cut off as soon as they have developed; they are left to dry for about a fortnight and may then be grown into separate plants in a cactus mixture.

Large plants may flower profusely throughout the summer; the deep orange-red flowers are truly magnificent.

Opuntia clavarioides is a very unusual species with cylindrical or club-shaped blue-grey joints resembling the fingers of a hand. This species, a native of Argentina, will thrive reasonably well, provided it is grafted. It is occasionally seen in flower.

OPUNTIA MICRODASYS (Rabbit's Ears)

Every cactus collection contains a number of Opuntia species. They occur from North America to the most southerly part of South America. Some species grow very tall (to 6 m—19 or 20 feet—and more). A few (e.g. O. polyacantha) may be left out of doors if they are given a sheltered position, which must not be too damp, particularly in winter.

Opuntia microdasys and O. rufida may be recommended to beginners. Both are compact species with, respectively, yellowish and reddish-brown tufts of very small spines, known as glochids. The albispina variety (*see* illustration) has tufts of white glochids. Care should be taken not to touch the tufts of glochids as they easily rub off into the skin and are unpleasant and difficult to remove.

Opuntia cacti require nutritious soil, adequate water and sun in the growing season. In winter they should be given a well-lit, dry situation in a temperature of about 8 °C.

Oreocereus neocelsianus

Oroya peruviana

OREOCEREUS NEOCELSIANUS

This genus includes excellent species for living-room cultivation. Many of them originate on the plateaux of the Andes and consequently their most ideal growing conditions are plenty of sun, a high daytime temperature and a low temperature at night. All species will grow well from seed, but grafted specimens are more vigorous and are more easily kept through the winter.

Because of its woolly hairs Oreocereus neocelsianus is beautiful even when not flowering. The flowers appear at the top, but only in mature plants.

Oreocereus fossulatus, from Bolivia, also has striking hair formation. The flowers are brownish-pink in colour. Oreocereus trollii (The Old Man from the Andes) is slightly smaller and is more densely haired.

OROYA PERUVIANA

This cactus genus was named after La Oroya, a mining town in Peru. It occurs in central Peru at an altitude of about 4,000 m (13,000 feet), and is therefore practically winter-hardy, though this does not mean that you should leave it outside.

Oroya peruviana is the best known species; a number of subspecies are known which will not be discussed here. This vigorous cactus flowers readily—an additional recommendation to the amateur.

Partly because of its origin, Oroya requires soil mixed with plenty of gravel. In winter it should be kept as cool and well-lit as possible.

Oscularia deltoides

Pachyphytum oviferum

OSCULARIA DELTOIDES

Mature specimens of Oscularia deltoides often make fine hanging plants. Like the closely related Lampranthus and Delosperma species (at one time they were all called Mesembryanthemum), this succulent, a native of South Africa, may be grown out of doors in summer. The triangular leaves are beautifully bloomed and the fragrant small pink flowers (1 cm—$\frac{1}{2}$ in.—across) frequently appear in large numbers.

It is important to keep this plant dry in winter, for otherwise its shape will be affected and it will flower less profusely.

Oscularia is one of those plants rarely available at the florist's and is usually distributed among collectors in the form of cuttings. These readily root in sandy soil.

PACHYPHYTUM OVIFERUM

The various Pachyphytum species are very pure in shape; they have fine colouring and are often strikingly bloomed. They originate in Mexico, where on the whole nature has produced more prickly than smooth plants. Pachyphytum oviferum is the most attractive species and needs no description—the photograph speaks for itself.

However, in the case of Pachyphytum bracteosum some elucidation is required. This succulent may grow to 50 cm (20 in.) in height and has inversely egg-shaped spatulate leaves, covered in violet bloom. Red flowers appear in summer.

Pachyphytum species must be kept cool and in good light in winter. In summer a cold greenhouse, or a spot close to the window is best.

Pachyveria 'Glauca'

Parodia microsperma

PACHYVERIA HYBRID

This succulent is the result of a love affair between Pachyphytum and Echeveria. In appearance it mainly resembles the latter.

A very well-known form is × Pachyveria 'Glauca', probably the outcome of crossing an Echeveria species with Pachyphytum compactum. It is a beautiful strain and deserves a place in every collection.

Another form in cultivation is 'Scheideckeri' (a cross between Pachyphytum bracteosum and Echeveria secunda). It has blue-green, spatulate leaves, covered in white bloom, and an unbranching inflorescence; the flowers are orange-red in colour. Other good strains are 'Clavata' and 'Clavifolia'. Pachyverias require the same care as Pachyphytum and Echeveria.

PARODIA MICROSPERMA

The genus Parodia embraces a few dozen species, occurring in Argentina, Brazil, Paraguay and Bolivia. As a rule they are globular in shape, but occasionally they acquire a cylindrical form. They are densely spined, but as a rule are not particularly beautiful. However, they have the advantage that they flower from an early age (even three-year-old seedlings may do so) and have a prolonged flowering season.

Parodia microsperma originates in northern Argentina; it is spherical in shape and grows to 10 cm (4 in.) in diameter. The flowers are very fine.

Parodia maassii has red flowers and long, hooked spines, a characteristic found in many species. P. aureispina also has hooked spines; these are golden-yellow in colour, as are the flowers.

Parodia nivosa   *Pelecyphora aselliformis*

PARODIA NIVOSA

Chalky soil, rich in humus, and mixed with about 25 per cent of sharp sand or stone-dust, is best for Parodia species. Make sure that they are not too damp; the root-neck is particularly sensitive. They like a sunny situation, but tolerate some shade. In winter they must not be kept in too cold an environment (12°C). Parodia species do not grow very quickly, at least not on their own roots. Grafting encourages growth.

Parodia nivosa owes its name to its snowy white spines (nivosa = snowy). You can imagine its beauty when its blood-red flowers appear; the photograph proves it. This species grows wild in northern Argentina.

PELECYPHORA ASELLIFORMIS

Aselliformis means 'like a sow-bug *or* wood-louse' and the plant has been so named because the areoles, i.e. the places where the spines develop, resemble this small crustacean.

This club-shaped little cactus may be a real ornament in your collection. Fairly small purple flowers appear at the top.

Pelecyphora pseudopectinata is more delicate in structure; its flowers are pinky-white with brown-striped petals.

Pelecyphora species are fairly difficult to cultivate. They grow slowly and require a very well-lit position. Be sure not to water too generously. It is frequently advised to add 25 per cent of sand to the normal soil mixture.

Pereskia aculeata 'Godseffiana'

Pereskiopsis spathulata (with grafted scion)

PERESKIA ACULEATA (Barbados Gooseberry)

If there is one plant in this book which does not look like a cactus at all, it must surely be Pereskia aculeata. It does, however, have spines; these are placed in pairs along the thin stems. This species, a native of the West Indies and Central America, is regarded as a forerunner of the typical cacti.

It is chiefly known as stock on which to graft other cacti, especially Epiphyllum species. Although it is sometimes considered not very decorative, the fine bronze foliage colour of the cultivar 'Godseffiana', which is enhanced by sunlight, and the fact that it is easy to grow, make it an excellent house plant.

Grow them in a sunny spot, keep the soil-ball adequately moist and cut back the over-long shoots of mature plants. These shoots may be used as cuttings to grow new plants.

PERESKIOPSIS SPATHULATA

Like Pereskia, Pereskiopsis is used as stock (*see* illustration). Slow-growing seedlings are grafted on its leaf-bearing shoots; union will take place within a few days. The advantage of this method is that the seedlings will grow much more rapidly and will therefore flower sooner.

This cactus looks rather like 'another' succulent. The inconspicuous spines are, in fact, thin and limp. The plant's relationship with Opuntia species is indicated chiefly by the flowers, which in the case of P. spathulata are red or yellow and about 3 cm (1 in.) across.

The plant is easy to grow. Plenty of moisture and a nutritious soil mixture rich in humus are essential conditions. Do not put it in too cold a spot in winter.

Pleiospilos longibracteata

Pyrrhocactus floccosus

PLEIOSPILOS LONGIBRACTEATA

Several Pleiospilos species occur in the eastern part of the Karroo in South Africa. These plants, usually fairly small, belong to the so-called ultra-succulents. Many species have completely adapted themselves to their extremely arid environment. The two leaves are practically spherical in shape, so that the area of evaporation is restricted to a minimum (P. nelii and P. bolusii). However, there are other species which have flattened leaves (*see* illustration).

Many plants closely resemble their stony environment in colour and shape, which makes them inconspicuous, hence the popular name 'mimicry plants'. The large yellowish flowers appear in late summer and autumn.

During the actual growing season (May–June) they should be watered fairly generously.

PYRRHOCACTUS FLOCCOSUS

This genus includes about ten species, originating in Argentina. They are fine, spherical cacti with vigorous, closely packed spines in the colours grey, grey-brown, nearly black and reddish-brown.

They are slow-growing and are known for their delicate root system. They should therefore not be kept in too cold an environment in winter. These cacti are not suitable for beginners; they grow best if grafted on stock. A porous soil mixture is essential. Some collectors grow these plants in soil mixed with 50–60 per cent of crushed bricks.

P. strausianus, P. paucicostatus and P. recondita are other well-known species.

Rebutia marsoneri

Rebutia senilis

REBUTIA MARSONERI

Rebutias occur in Argentina and Bolivia, where they often grow at altitudes of several thousand metres (above 10,000 feet); they therefore tolerate fairly low temperatures and consequently should be kept at 6–8 °C in winter. Of course their situation should be well-lit and dry. If cared for in this manner, these dwarf cacti will flower profusely.

Dozens of species and varieties are known. The species illustrated above, discovered in 1935 by Blossfeld and Marsoner, caused a sensation among cactus growers, for all the species known up till then produced reddish flowers.

Rebutia marsoneri is one of the largest of these dwarf cacti. It will grow reasonably well on its own root system, but will do even better if grafted on Eriocereus jusbertii stock.

REBUTIA SENILIS

Rebutias are known for their prolific flowering. The flowers frequently develop near the base of the stems, usually in spring. These small cacti are particularly suitable for 'window-sill' collectors.

Rebutia senilis with its conspicuous white spine formation is certainly worth growing. A very attractive species is the smallest of all, Rebutia pygmaea, which has orange flowers. A very popular one is Rebutia minuscula, which produces medium-sized red flowers.

In very warm weather it is advisable to syringe these plants frequently. Apart from this, an airy position, screened from bright sunlight, is essential. They will thrive on the window-sill, but also in a glass-covered cold frame outside. These cacti readily form seed which may be used for propagation.

Rhipsalidopsis gaertneri

Rhipsalidopsis × graeseri

RHIPSALIDOPSIS GAERTNERI (Easter Cactus)

At first sight Schlumbergera and Rhipsalidopsis are very similar. Both might be called jointed cacti, for their stems are conspicuously divided into joints. However, as their names, Christmas cactus and Easter cactus, indicate, they flower at different times of the year.

This beautiful epiphyte starts to flower in April–May and continues for at least 6–8 weeks.

Vigorous specimens are usually grafted on Pereskia or Eriocereus. Fully grown joints may be easily rooted, but as you know, they will grow much less vigorously on their own roots.

RHIPSALIDOPSIS × GRAESERI

This hybrid (also called Epiphyllopsis) is the result of a courtship between the Easter cactus mentioned above and its relative Rhipsalidopsis rosea which, as its name indicates, has pink flowers. As far as the colour of its flowers is concerned, the hybrid comes halfway between its two parents: orange-red to lilac-pink.

Both Easter cactus forms require humid warmth during the growing period. Occasional spray-misting encourages growth. They must be screened from bright sunlight; a half-shady position is best. Give a little more water from August to December, but from January onwards keep fairly dry in the best possible light. Maintain the temperature at 10–14 °C; this will encourage bud formation. Turn the plant as little as possible to prevent the buds dropping. As soon as these have formed increase the water supply.

Rhipsalis houlletiana   *Rochea coccinea 'Variegata'*

RHIPSALIS HOULLETIANA

There are quite a few Rhipsalis species; most of them originate in South America. Like Schlumbergera, Epiphyllum and Rhipsalidopsis, the majority are epiphytes. The flowers are small, but usually appear in large numbers. After flowering, creamy, yellow, pink or red berries develop; these continue to decorate the plant for a long time.

Rhipsalis likes shade and a certain degree of warmth. The soil must be rich in humus. In summer fairly generous watering is essential. Never place the plants in the sun. A resting period in winter, during which very little water should be given, makes good sense. If they are kept in heated rooms in winter, the soil must not dry out.

Another interesting species of this genus is Rhipsalis pachyptera, which has red-tipped yellow flowers.

ROCHEA COCCINEA

This house plant is a native of South Africa. The fact that it is rarely seen may be due to the short period during which it is marketed (May–June); it is also possible that it is considered too stiff a plant to be attractive. It is nevertheless quite distinctive in habit: it has straight stems closely covered in short leaves.

The bright red flowers grow in umbels at the top of the stems. They will appear in abundance only if you remember that Rochea species are typical 'cold' plants, that is, plants which flower only if kept very cool and dry in winter. A temperature of 5–6 °C is adequate.

The variegated form is a rarity.

Sansevieria cylindrica   *Sansevieria trifasciata 'Golden Hahnii'*

SANSEVIERIA CYLINDRICA

Of the more than 70 Sansevieria species only Sansevieria trifasciata is cultivated on a reasonable scale. This is a pity, for there are others which deserve a place on the window-sill.

One of these is Sansevieria cylindrica, which occurs in tropical West Africa. This is actually a fibre plant of some commercial importance. However, its practically cylindrical leaves make it stand out in a collection of succulents.

It is cared for in the same way as the extremely well-known Sansevieria trifasciata, but it is not quite so hardy and tolerates little water, especially in winter.

SANSEVIERIA TRIFASCIATA (Mother-in-law's Tongue)

Many people consider this plant old-fashioned, stiff and ugly, but it is unthinkable that it should ever be entirely rejected. It is certainly easily cared for. Provided it is protected against bright sunlight, it will maintain its colouring. Make sure it does not suffer from the cold in winter. Apart from this it tolerates an extremely dry and airless atmosphere.

As well as the typical variety of the species, the 'Laurentii' strain is well-known. This cultivar is distinguished by its creamy longitudinal stripes. 'Hahnii', 'Golden Hahnii' and 'Silver Hahnii' are other well-known varieties; these are probably permanent dwarf forms. They have become very popular, especially in recent years.

In summer they should be watered adequately; keep them dry in winter. Mature specimens may produce flowers: these are slightly fragrant and are greenish-white in colour. The inflorescence is spike-shaped.

Sedum pachyphyllum

Sedum rubrotinctum

SEDUM PACHYPHYLLUM

This species is one of the Sedums most frequently used as a house plant. Like most others, it is very easy to grow. The yellow flowers appear in spring.

The finest Sedum species is S. morganianum. The strikingly pale grey leaves grow on trailing stems which may grow to as much as 50 cm (20 in.). The pink inflorescence is inconspicuous.

Another attractive species is Sedum stahlii. This plant has extremely thin stems covered in small, oval green leaves; these turn brown particularly in sunlight. The yellow flowers grow in small racemes.

Other valuable forms are S. palmeri and S. lineare 'Variegatum'.

SEDUM RUBROTINCTUM

Most Sedum species used as house plants are natives of Mexico, but the origin of Sedum rubrotinctum is uncertain. This beautiful and popular species puts forth racemes of yellow flowers in summer. The fine reddish-brown colour develops especially if the plants receive plenty of sunlight. A cultivar called 'Aureum' has unusual pink to salmon-coloured leaves.

Sedum species must be put in the best available light. From June to August they may be placed out of doors. In winter they are kept in a cool position, but they also tolerate a warmer environment. Do not hesitate to water fairly generously in summer.

The plants are easily propagated from cuttings rooted in a sandy mixture. Detached leaves also root easily.

Sedum sieboldii 'Mediovariegatum'

Selenicereus species

SEDUM SIEBOLDII

The Sedum genus embraces many species: about 500, according to some experts. It would be very interesting to see the entire collection together. Various wild species occur in this country, while innumerable forms are grown in our gardens. They grow wild in the Alps, the Pyrenees, Asia Minor, the United States and elsewhere.

One species is used indoors as well as in the garden, namely S. sieboldii. This native of Japan has fine, circular leaves and red flowers which frequently appear in the middle of winter. After flowering, early in spring, the flower remnants are removed and at the same time the plant is re-potted. Use normal potting compost. A sunny position is desirable. 'Mediovariegatum' is a beautiful strain with yellow blotches in the centre of the leaves.

SELENICEREUS GRANDIFLORUS (Queen of the Night)

A number of Selenicereus species occur from Texas southwards. With their long, thin stems they climb high into the trees, attaching themselves by aerial roots.

Selenicereus requires a soil mixture rich in humus and a position in light shade. Since it is a very large plant, it must be grown in a roomy pot and be supported by a wooden framework. The flowers of the best known species, Selenicereus grandiflorus, are very large: they grow up to 25 cm (10 in.) in length ånd 30 cm (12 in.) across. They are very fragrant and appear at night, opening for a few hours only. By next morning the flowers have wilted.

Senecio haworthii

Stapelia variegata

SENECIO HAWORTHII

Most collectors of succulents know this plant by the name Kleinia tomentosa. The name is appropriate, for tomentosa means 'felty' and in fact the entire plant is covered in felty white hairs. When watering be careful not to let the foliage get wet, for otherwise the plant would lose much of its beauty.

In Senecio rowleyanus the leaves are transformed into small, bead-like organs. These 'beads' grow on thin, limp, and consequently trailing, stems.

Another form worth mentioning is Senecio stapeliiformis, a species with stems shaped like those of Stapelia. This plant has beautiful orange-red tubular flowers.

STAPELIA VARIEGATA (Variegated Carrion Flower)

This very peculiar plant was introduced to this part of the world as early as the beginning of the 17th century. The name carrion flower is based on the fact that its disagreeable odour attracts blow flies which, as the result of the ingenious structure of the flowers, take the lumps of pollen to other flowers, thus effecting cross-pollination.

As a rule the flowers of Stapelia variegata are greenish- or sulphur-yellow, with numerous dark reddish-brown blotches, but the colour varies considerably.

In the period April–June a few stems may be detached from mature plants; these are allowed to dry before being inserted in sharp sand. They root readily and may then be potted in nutritious soil.

Stenocereus chichipe

Stetsonia coryne

STENOCEREUS CHICHIPE

These cacti, sometimes called Lemaireocereus, may grow to 10 m (32 feet) in height. Naturally this will not happen in your living-room or your greenhouse, but only in its native country which, again, is Mexico. They will not produce flowers, since as house plants they remain too small to do so. Nevertheless they are beautiful in shape and colour and, being vigorous, soon provide us with well-grown specimens.

They like porous soil. In summer they should be placed in a sunny spot and watered fairly freely. In winter they must be kept dry and not too cold.

Particularly fine species are: Stenocereus chichipe (*see* illustration), S. thurberi (rather difficult to grow), S. pruinosus and S. dumortieri.

STETSONIA CORYNE

As a rule this species is difficult to grow on its own root system. It is usually grafted on Eriocereus jusbertii and will then grow satisfactorily.

This cactus owes its specific name coryne to the club-shaped stems formed by young plants (coryne = club). At a later stage they grow into unbranched columns. In this part of the world they rarely flower, but in their native Argentina they produce white flowers, 15 cm (6 in.) in length. The plant is worth growing for its own sake: its stems, initially blue, later turning green, are covered in fairly long thorns, eventually grey in colour.

This species may be grown in the normal soil mixture. Water normally and of course keep dry in winter; the temperature should not be too low.

Trichocereus santiaguensis   *Trichocereus terscheckii*

TRICHOCEREUS SANTIAGUENSIS

The numerous species of this genus are found in Chile, Ecuador, Argentina and Bolivia. Some grow into trees, others are of creeping habit. They are columnar cacti, whose flowers frequently appear at night; in that case they are white. Other species flower during the day in varying colours.

Trichocereus are excellent plants for collectors; they are in demand among growers because some of them provide good grafting stock.

One of these is T. spachianus, a native of western Argentina. Another species used as stock is T. pachanoi, which grows in the Andes at an altitude of 3,000 m (9,750 feet) and therefore tolerates low temperatures.

TRICHOCEREUS TERSCHECKII

In summer Trichocereus species require a very sunny position and may be placed in a sheltered spot outside. During the winter they may be kept practically dry. They are undemanding as regards soil: almost any mixture will do.

Larger species grow too big for use in the living-room, but young specimens, grown as long as possible in small pots, are quite satisfactory.

Trichocereus schickendantzii is better known than the species illustrated, which is not often cultivated. It is an attractive plant which in cultivation grows to about 50 cm (20 in.), but rarely flowers. Trichocereus species are easily grown from seed.

Yucca aloifolia

Schlumbergera × buckleyi

YUCCA ALOIFOLIA

The Yucca has become very well known in recent years. It is found in many domestic interiors, in shop windows and in offices. The plants are usually imported from southern countries and are relatively expensive. Although it is a xerophyte (i.e. a plant which tolerates drought), Yucca is actually not a succulent. It is undemanding, but does require a well-lit situation. In summer water fairly freely and feed regularly. The plants are quite insensitive to a dry atmosphere.

The lower, thick and leathery, leaves (they are sword-shaped) constantly turn unsightly and are best removed with scissors. In the course of time the plant thus becomes tree-shaped.

I believe it is inadvisable to buy this plant if there are small children in the house, for the leaf-tips are very sharp. (Yucca elephantipes has soft leaves.)

SCHLUMBERGERA × BUCKLEYI (Christmas Cactus)

To obtain a profusely flowering Christmas cactus it is necessary to take several advance measures. To begin with it is best to buy a grafted specimen. Next you should give the plant two resting periods, one in the autumn and another after flowering. During the first resting season water very sparingly and do not feed. When the flower-buds become visible, increase the water supply. When the plant is in bud or in flower it must not be moved. After flowering the plant should be allowed to rest on its laurels for at least a month.

The Christmas cactus likes soil rich in humus, a shady situation and fairly generous watering, except, of course, in the resting periods.

It is nowadays thought to be a hybrid between Crab cactus (S. truncata) and a related species, S. russellianus, both of which occur wild in the forests of S.E. Brazil.

BIBLIOGRAPHY

Backeberg, C.   Das Kakteenlexicon.
                                   VEB Gustav Fischer Verlag, Jena.

Bloom, E. V.   Collectors' Cacti.
                                   W. H. & L. Collingridge Ltd., London.

Boarder, A.   Starting with Cacti.
                                   W. H. & L. Collingridge Ltd., London.

Borg, J.   Cacti. A Gardener's Handbook for their Identification and
                                   Cultivation.
                                   Blandford Press, London.

Ginns, R.   Cacti and other Succulents.
                                   Penguin Books.

Herwig, R. and   The Complete Book of Houseplants.
Schubert, M. (transl. M. Powell)   Lutterworth Press.

Higgins, V.   Succulents in Cultivation.
                                   Blandford Press, London.

Higgins, V.   The Study of Cacti.
                                   Blandford Press, London.

Jacobsen, H.   Lexicon of Succulent Plants.
(transl. L. Glass)   Blandford Press, London.

Lamb, E. & B.   Pocket Encyclopaedia of Cacti in Colour.
                                   Blandford Press, London.

Leese, O. & M.   Desert Plants: Cacti & Succulents.
                                   W. H. & L. Collingridge Ltd., London.

Martin, M. J., Chapman   Cacti and their cultivation.
P. R. & Auger, H. A.   Faber & Faber.

Subik, R. &   Decorative Cacti. A Guide to Succulent House Plants.
Kaplicka Jirina.   Spring Books. Hamlyn Publishing Group, London.
(transl. O. Kuthanova)

INDEX OF PLANTS